OLD DOG,
NEW
Understanding and
Retraining Elderly
and Rescued Dogs
TRICKS

David Taylor

OLD DOG, NEW TRICKS

Understanding and Retraining Elderly and Rescued Dogs

CASSELL
ILLUSTRATED

This book is dedicated to my granddaughters, Aphra and Julia Pilkington.

First published in Great Britain in 2006 by Cassell Illustrated,
a division of Octopus Publishing Group Limited,
2–4 Heron Quays, Canary Wharf, London, E14 4JP

Text copyright © 2006 David Taylor
Design and layout © Cassell Illustrated

A CIP catalogue record for this book is available from the British Library.

ISBN-13: 978-1-844034-43-7
ISBN-10: 1-844034-43-7

10 9 8 7 6 5 4 3 2 1

Printed in China

CONTENTS

If you pick up a starving dog and make him prosperous, he will not bite you. That is the principal difference between a dog and a man.
MARK TWAIN

INTRODUCTION

So you and your household are taking on board a new pet in the shape of an adult, perhaps even an old adult, dog. The other day a taxi-driver described to me how he had recently adopted a 10-year-old male Rottweiler when the previous owner, his mother-in-law, was admitted to a hospice and unlikely ever to leave. 'A most gentle dog with people,' he explained (Rottweilers do indeed often belie their popular reputation). 'But incredibly strong and with only one apparent fault – a murderous attitude to any other dog he comes across!' I can easily imagine his problem.

Adopting an older dog occurs frequently and for a variety of reasons – the death of a friend or relative; a visit to the animal shelter where your heart goes out to the greyhound abandoned when his racing days came to an end; or to the mutt that is due to be euthanased in a week's time unless someone gives him a good home, and, of course, there is the dog who walks into your life, literally, up the garden path, a seemingly ownerless vagrant, and then proceeds to hang around indefinitely.

Of course it is utterly right and proper to give a home to these mature foundlings, but such animals can bring a lot of 'baggage' with them. They have had years of experience, good and perhaps bad, of which you may have no or little knowledge, and they may never have received effective training. There are several advantages in giving a home to a mature dog: he is usually house-trained, he has a developed, stable personality and he is unlikely to suffer from puppyhood-type disease.

As with some elderly human beings, they can be set in their ways, averse to change and, all too often, inclined to bad, or at least undesirable, habits. The loss of their old family, equivalent to being ejected from the pack, may cause them to feel insecure, and some behavioural problems may only surface a few weeks after arriving in their new home. Nevertheless, to have a dog as a pet is a delight, a privilege and a distinct benefit to your health and well-being. Just stroking a dog has been shown to lower our blood pressure, and recently the NHS in some areas has begun prescribing pet dogs for patients as a valuable adjunct to medication.

The vagaries of fate may, however, deposit a puppy or young dog in your lap. To some extent you will have a 'clean sheet' to work on in educating the animal in the ways of your family and general good behaviour, but there can be difficulties even with these immature dogs, particularly if they were not handled well in the first few weeks or months of life. The vast majority of behavioural problems, such as aggression towards people, house soiling and destructiveness, are to be found in dogs under nine years of age.

Things have got to change, you will say. Your new dog must fit in with your regime and that of your family. How, though, do you go about it? Your main aim must be to understand your dog, to learn about 'what makes him tick'. An informed relationship with a much loved pet can be one of the most special in your life. Mentally, dogs aren't so complex as human beings but, nevertheless, every dog is an individual with thoughts and a personality of his own.

Obviously dogs are dogs, different in a multitude of ways from people, cats or crocodiles. So what *are* dogs? Where have they come from? Even if you know virtually nothing about your newly acquired dog's curriculum vitae, learning more about the biology and position of dogs within the animal kingdom can help us to understand something of the way in which they think and act as they do.

EVOLUTION OF THE DOMESTIC DOG

1

The dog belongs to the family of dog-like animals called *Canidae*, pack hunters (unlike the vast majority of species of *Felidae*, the cat family) of which other members are foxes, wolves, jackals, coyotes and wild hunting dogs. Some of these look like the dog whereas others are very different, but all the wild Canids have certain things in common – long narrow heads with long jaws and plentiful teeth. The cheek teeth are specially designed, partly for slicing and partly for grinding, and can efficiently handle both carnivorous and vegetarian diets. The multi-purpose dental structure of *Canidae* is one of their admirable qualities, and has enabled them to spread so widely across the planet and to survive in a variety of habitats from arid deserts to the freezing Arctic, from tundra to jungle to the mountain forests of Northern regions.

Only artificially selective breeding at the hands of human beings over comparatively recent centuries has created some breeds of domestic dog that are built differently and look quite unlike their wild cousins.

ANCESTORS

The wolf, fox and jackal have each been claimed as the domestic dog's direct ancestor. In the nineteenth century, Charles Darwin was one of those who, observing the great diversity of dog breeds, championed the belief that more than one wild ancestor had been involved. Nowadays, most scientists dispute this and believe the direct ancestor is likely to have been an animal similar to the grey wolf (*Canis lupus*).

Around 60 million years ago, in the Palaeocene epoch, when the last of the dinosaurs were making their exit, and the first small, furry and rather unpromising looking mammals were to be found, a weasel-like animal with a long, flexible body, long tail and short legs lived in the forests. This was *Miacis*, the earliest ancestor not only of canids but also of other families: bears, weasels, racoons, civets, hyenas and cats. It walked, like a modern bear, on the soles of its feet (not like modern dogs which walk on 'the tips of their toes'). These feet had five well separated digits but a flat-footed gait is not very useful when pursuing fast-moving prey. Flat foots can't catch fleet foots!

Miacis had the distinctive teeth of a carnivore. Its brain, though small, was significantly bigger than those of the other primitive carnivores living at the time, the creodonts. These, while far more plentiful in numbers than *Miacis*, did not play a part in the evolution of

WOLVES

Wolves are highly sociable animals among their own kind. Pack size can be between two and 20 in number, the average in most habitats being around a dozen. The animals hunt together, share food, both with each other as well with their young, and males will assist in feeding cubs. This 'family-friendly' attitude was passed down to the domestic dog. You, as a pet-owner, must accept that you are a member of your dog's pack and must act accordingly if you are to understand its behaviour in and around the home.

Strange but true: only 40 genes separate these wild wolves from domesticated dogs such as Pugs and Poodles.

the dog and finally became extinct about 20 million years ago. Brain size had begun to show itself as a powerful evolutionary advantage.

By the early Oligocene epoch, about 35 million years ago, *Miacis* had given rise to a wide variety of early canids. Some were bear-like dogs, others hyena-like dogs and others, most remarkable of all, were cat-like dogs! But it was yet another type, the dog-like dogs, that was the only one destined to survive. Snoopy and Lassie and Deputy Dawg were on their way!

Over the millennia that followed, the size of the canid brains gradually increased and by the late Miocene epoch, 10–15 million years ago, we find fossils of *Tomarctus*, an animal that, while not having the degree of intelligence of the dog, seems to have displayed all its social instincts.

The first true *Canis* came on the scene between five and seven million years ago. It was beginning to walk on four of its toes (the fifth was to become the dew claw) and had a more tightly compact foot – much better for chasing prey.

Finally, one million years ago, an early wolf, the Etruscan, was to be found roaming Eurasia. Recent studies suggest that the Etruscan wolf was almost certainly the direct ancestor of the domestic dog as well as of present-day wolves. One small subspecies of wolf, *Canis lupus pallipes*, now found in the Middle East and India, is considered to be closer to the dog than any other wolf subspecies. As with the domestic cat, it seems to be the case that the original forebears of the domestic dog lived in the Middle East.

Brain size with consequent powers of intelligence, great adaptability and a social organization within packs that provided co-operation and mutual support were the principal advantages of the wolf. In due course these became, for their descendants, the canine qualities so important in forging unique relationships with mankind.

ARTIFICIAL SELECTION

The first domestication of the dog occurred at least 10,000, perhaps as much as 35,000, years ago. It may all have begun with wolves scavenging in the middens of human habitations, or perhaps the first close contact between humans and wolves was when early man hunted the animals for food and took pups away for fattening up. In due course, wandering bands of *Homo sapiens* brought the creature with them from the Middle East to Europe. Similarly, man imported an ancestor of the dingo into Australia. Domestic dogs spread rapidly across the world, establishing themselves everywhere except in Antarctica. They were man's earliest animal companions.

Small sculptures of dogs with curled tails dating from about 6500 BC have been discovered in Iraq, and domestic dog bones from an earlier period in the Stone Age (about 7500 BC) have been found in Yorkshire. Similar finds have been recorded from 10,000-year-old cave sediments in Czechoslovakia. The oldest domestic dog remains unearthed in the United States were found at Jaguar Cave, a Stone Age Native American site in Idaho, and were dated at around 8300 BC. Fossils of two kinds of dog, medium and large, were discovered there.

Breeding of dogs began very soon after their first domestication. They were bred for their usefulness – as hunting assistants, guards and to provide meat and fur. In time dogs became more specialized and were selected and bred for particular tasks. Artificial selection by man took over from the natural selection that Nature had employed in their wild ancestors for all those millions of years.

Sight hounds
One of the earliest groups to emerge was the kind of hunting dog known as a 'sight hound' or 'gaze hound'.

The intent gaze, lithe body and athletic legs of this Whippet are typical of the sight hound.

This tough but good-natured Arctic dog, the Norwegian Elkhound, is a very ancient breed of scent hound historically used to hunt moose, elk and, sometimes, wolves.

They first appeared on the scene about 6,000 years ago. Examples of modern breeds of this type are the Afghan Hound, Saluki and Greyhound. These dogs were invaluable when hunting quarry in the desert or treeless savannah. Swift and silent, sometimes aided by trained falcons, these hounds would harry, distract and run down deer and gazelle that were beyond the range of bow, spear or javelin. Exported from their Middle Eastern birthplace, they gave rise to such breeds as the Russian Borzoi, Scottish Deerhound, Irish Wolfhound and the Whippet.

Scent hounds

Much later, man developed the sniffers, the scent hounds. Distinctly European breeds, these were marathon runners rather than sprinters, able to follow a scent trail and with the stamina to run the quarry to eventual exhaustion. Some scent hounds would then kill the prey; others were trained to keep it at bay and attract the huntsman by 'giving tongue' – baying. An example of this type of breed is the Norwegian Elkhound.

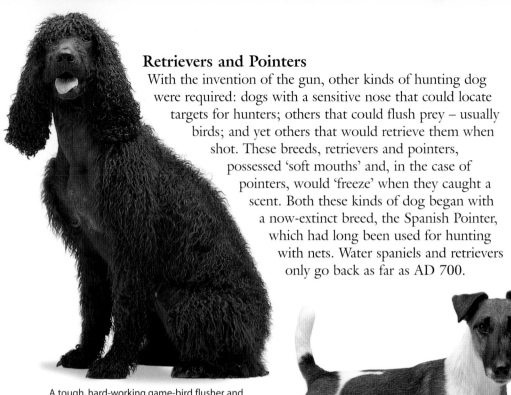

Retrievers and Pointers

With the invention of the gun, other kinds of hunting dog were required: dogs with a sensitive nose that could locate targets for hunters; others that could flush prey – usually birds; and yet others that would retrieve them when shot. These breeds, retrievers and pointers, possessed 'soft mouths' and, in the case of pointers, would 'freeze' when they caught a scent. Both these kinds of dog began with a now-extinct breed, the Spanish Pointer, which had long been used for hunting with nets. Water spaniels and retrievers only go back as far as AD 700.

A tough, hard-working game-bird flusher and retriever, the Irish Water Spaniel is equally at home on dry land or on water.

The Smooth Fox Terrier was originally employed as an expert hunter of rats.

Terriers

Another type of hunting dog with a very different physique and temperament was developed, for some reason largely in Britain, to tackle burrowing quarry – foxes, rabbits, badgers and rats. They were already there when the Romans arrived, and they described them as terrarii, creatures of the earth, from which our name 'terrier' comes. Their principal attributes were, and are, short legs, smallish, compact bodies and a fiery, tenacious spirit. A ragbag of tough underground-working dogs for centuries, they became very popular in the late eighteenth and nineteenth centuries, particularly among the working classes of the new industrial centres, such as miners and quarry men.

Utility dogs

As man's activities diversified, other dogs became specialized as guard-dogs, war-dogs, sledge-dogs and beasts of burden. Dogs could rescue drowning people, guide them through snowy mountains, alert them to intruders, run alongside horse-drawn carriages, track down criminals, sniff out explosives and, nowadays, drugs, and guide the blind or assist the deaf.

Sadly, the St Bernard with its barrel of spirits no longer accompanies monks in rescuing lost and freezing travellers.

Quick thinking and the ability to calculate tactics are essential in herding dogs such as the Border Collie.

Herding dogs

Once other animals, such as cattle, sheep and goats, had been domesticated, other breeds of dog were gradually developed to assist man in his farming. The dog's usefulness as a herder became apparent. The innate tactics that its ancestor, the wolf, would use to separate a target victim from the herd were exploited in the sheepdog.

Companion breeds

But forget these hard-working animals. For over at least 2000 years another type of dog, of which the Pekingese is a good example, has been developed independently both in Europe and the Far East. These are the completely idle 'toy breeds', dogs that provide companionship, affection and

Fancy breeds such as this Pekingese play a valuable role in keeping people happy and providing companionship.

amusement for their human companions. They do no work. Many are truly 'lap dogs'. But their contribution to human happiness is real and highly significant. With them miniaturization was an important feature, though in many the extremes of size were achieved only quite recently. Once the preserve of kings and aristocracy, 'toy' breeds are now kept in enormous numbers by people in all walks of life.

Modern breeds

Despite the millennia involved in producing the modern domestic dog, it is nevertheless fascinating to remember that most of today's 400 or so recognizable breeds were established after 1850. The rise in popularity of dog shows and breeding for the show bench is the explanation. Now, for good or ill, we have entered the age of the 'designer dog', where artificial selection meets the world of fad and fashion. Enter the Labradoodle, a clever, easily-trained, happy-go-lucky dog that is especially good with children, the Black Russian Terrier, a fearless but not aggressive guard dog needing a firm hand, early socialization and plenty of training, as well as a range of Wolfdogs.

HUMANS, WOLVES AND DOGS

It is important and fascinating when faced with problems of human/dog interaction to see what can be learnt from looking at the similarities in the social relationships of the dog, the wolf from which it is descended and the human being, with whom it becomes, hopefully, a loved and loving family member.

The problem for feral dogs with living in groups is that there may be less food available for each individual when out scavenging. Like human tramps, feral dogs also tend, for much of the time, to drift through life alone except, of course, for the odd social encounter which may or may not result in the sharing of food. With no set routine or guaranteed food source, feral dogs, like feral human beings, become accustomed and attuned to the ways of non-domestic survival, though they are not permanently mentally damaged in any way. Consequently, it is difficult, but not impossible, with much patience, re-training and understanding to bring long-abandoned dogs back into the home environment.

From time to time the subject of so-called 'wolf children' comes up in the media. Are such feral human beings anything more than the stuff of legend – Romulus and Remus or Kipling's Mowgli, for example? Children who have been abandoned by their parents, rejected by society for whatever reason, may on rare occasions be taken in by a group, not just of wolves but also, according to reliable reports, dogs, goats, monkeys and even bears.

One of the most famous cases was that in 1920 of two Indian girls, Kamala and Amala, who were found in remote countryside west of Calcutta living with wolves and two wolf cubs in a den. Kamala was thought to be about five years of age and Amala around two. The girls ate raw meat, howled and moved about on all fours. They could run faster in this manner than a person on two legs. Their senses of hearing and vision were unusually sharp. Amala died within a year of being found while Kamala lived to her teens, but never learned more than three dozen words.

Dogs, like their human owners, are highly sociable animals.

ARE WOLVES LIKE US?

In many ways wolves are like us. They are territorial, socializing, predatory animals living in fairly stable family/social groups who are happy to scavenge or to co-operate in hunting. Some members of the group go out searching for food while others remain at home caring for the youngsters and are supplied with meals brought back by the hunters. So, yes, in every respect they are very like us.

Both human and wolf societies are hierarchical. There is a distinct pecking order built of dominance-submission relationships that, when accepted by the vast majority of group members, makes for peaceful co-existence and co-operation and suppresses serious confrontations. Think of our society, its strata, its privileged and its underclass – very wolf-like.

In 1998 Ivan Mishukov was found living with a pack of feral dogs on the streets of Reutova, Russia. He could talk as he had learned to do so before being thrown out by alcoholic parents. Even more recently, in 2001, a ten-year-old boy, Alex Rivas, was discovered near Talcahuano, Chile. He had lived in a cave with stray dogs for two years, at first suckling from a bitch that had recently given birth, and then going out at night with them on scavenging expeditions.

Feral and roaming dogs

Most of the dogs we see running around our towns, apparently without benefit of owner, are, in fact, owned dogs which are unwisely permitted to roam. But there are also numbers of truly feral dogs in our cities: ownerless, vagrant, rough-living animals. Do they revert to their ancestral wolf pack-type habits? Surprisingly, it appears that they are not particularly sociable. Most of these canine tramps are solitary drifters, and groups of more than two are rarely sighted. Bigger groups of dogs are usually owned, with homes close to one another. They behave, in fact, like a bunch of young teenagers living in the same street or block of flats.

Both owned and truly feral, roaming dogs are territorial in the sense of having home ranges normally centred on their sleeping places but they are not defended in the manner of many truly territorial animal species. Punch-ups are rarely seen between feral dogs and when they do occur it is generally not about territory but because of unfamiliarity. For dogs and wolves but thankfully not, in this case, humans, familiarity, knowing who's who, distinguishing friend and family from stranger, is very important and to a large extent is based on odour. To that end, these animals enthusiastically indulge in urine marking within sight of other individuals, sniff urine traces and thrust their noses under one another's tails. Mere human nostrils cannot decipher the highly complex information contained in a damp patch on a lamp post – or, as we shall discuss later, on your expensive Persian rug.

Imprinting
An important factor in man's domestication of the wolf was the process known as imprinting which occurs in the early days of life of the young of wolves, dogs and many other mammals and birds. This is the forming of a powerful bond between the youngster and some other individual or individuals, which, of course, frequently includes its parents. This attachment only occurs during a fairly short period not long after birth; in the case of dogs it is between the third and fourteenth weeks of life. The effects of imprinting persist, however. The bond between a wolf cub and human beings – its family, its pack – oiled the wheels of domestication. Bonded to its humans it would follow them, stick by them and, crucially perhaps, loyally defend the homestead. The modern dog behaves in a similar way.

Wolf characteristics
Surprisingly, perhaps, with the passing of millennia the characteristics of the wolf are still to be found even in the fanciest pedigree breeds of the modern Kennel Club. In the 1960s, a German scientist, Dr Zimen, studied and compared the behaviour of a pack of wolves and a large group of poodles kept in adjoining enclosures. He found that the wolves exhibited 362 distinct behaviours, 64 per cent of which were exhibited in identical or at least very similar form by the poodles. Only 13 per cent of wolf behaviours, mainly to do with vocal and visual communication – thank goodness toy poodles don't howl under a full moon! – were no longer present in any form in the dogs. Perhaps children should chant not 'Who's afraid of the Big Bad Wolf?' but 'Who's afraid of the Fairly Bad Poodle?'

Man's best friend
How best to sum up the relationship between man and dog? There are numerous ways that

Having a pet is good for an owner's psychological and physical health.

we can benefit each other. Wolves and human beings are both social animals with a similar pack or society structure that involves cooperation, seeking and sharing food and sharing care for the young. Both form hierarchies within which individuals must adopt a place in the pecking order and both, yes we humans too, are predators.

GETTING A NEW DOG

2

The newly bequeathed, adopted or rescued dog is about to arrive in your home, and it is vital to consider how to smooth the entry of your new pet into the pack that you call your family. If, when acquiring a new dog, you have any choice in the matter, as when visiting the inmates of Battersea Dogs Home or your local RSPCA shelter, it is essential not to allow your heart to rule your head.

Consider what sort of dog would suit you and what sort of dog you would suit. No matter how winsome and appealing that forlorn-looking creature in kennel number three may be, you must think coolly and calmly. Is it a breed that needs plenty of exercise? Would it be happy living in a third-floor, garden-free flat on the High Street? Have you the time and motivation to thoroughly groom that long Afghan-type coat or attend regularly to all the nooks and crannies on a Spaniel's bodywork? Can you afford to feed a Great Dane? Why has that adorable pooch been in the shelter for so long? Find out whether it has been 'rehomed' once or perhaps several times already. If so, why did it return? Does it have some apparently intractable behaviour problem? Consider everything carefully and discuss matters with other family members and staff at the shelter before making your decision. Don't be tempted to adopt an appealing-looking dog with sad eyes without thinking through the consequences of your decision, or you may come to regret it.

DO YOUR RESEARCH

Obtain as much information as you can on the dog's history. Health records, vaccination certificates and pedigree forms (which should provide the actual date of birth) are important documents. You may also be able to speak to a relative, neighbour or vet with knowledge of the dog's life before you came on the scene. Obviously you can learn nothing about a walk-in 'refugee' but many dogs adopted from animal shelters or charities will often be accompanied by good paperwork.

THE DOG'S HEALTH

The health of the new dog is a primary consideration. Most dogs coming from animal shelters will be checked over by a vet before leaving while those from other sources, particularly old animals, are very much unknown quantities. With the latter it is highly advisable to arrange for your vet to give the newcomer a thorough examination as soon as possible.

Provide the vet with a sample (a teaspoonful is enough) of the dog's droppings so that they can be checked for the existence of parasites. Clearing a dog of parasites, such as round worms, has a fascinating additional advantage in many cases. Dogs that have difficulty remembering commands, or in learning in general, can improve significantly after being de-wormed.

If nothing is known about the dog's current vaccination status, it is best to take the precaution of having him re-vaccinated. There is no risk in this even if, unbeknown to you, the dog did have his booster shots very recently. The important vaccines are those against canine distemper, canine leptospirosis, canine viral hepatitis and, in some countries, rabies.

If the pet is known or thought to be on any sort of medication, for the control of arthritis, for example, seek veterinary advice. Don't use Grandma's pills on him even if she is a long-term martyr to rheumatism or whatever.

If you are thinking of taking on an elderly animal, you must be fully prepared to handle any ailments and afflictions, which, as with old people, are increasingly likely as the years pass. With degenerative conditions of the bony skeleton, such as arthritis, stiffening spines, and cartilage troubles in the knees or chronic heart disease, the owner is in it for the long haul. Medication may have to be given for months, if not years, and general management of the dog adjusted as necessary. Consider insuring your pet for veterinary treatment should it fall ill or have an accident. Older animals with chronic conditions as arthritis or heart problems can require expensive professional attention over a lengthy period of time, and the repair of a fractured limb or removal of a tumour may cost several hundred pounds in fees.

MAINTAIN THE ROUTINE

Obtain any information you can on the dog's previous feeding routine. If he had a favourite proprietary brand of food, getting a supply of it will help you to introduce him to unfamiliar surroundings and a new regime. Any changes you decide to make to the previous diet should be gradual. Similarly, obtain – if you can – any of his 'personal' belongings, such as his dog basket, feeding bowl or much-loved toy. The dog may be very attached to its familiar possessions and may be impelled to guard them obsessively. In such cases, particularly if there is an existing family pet in the household, it may be best to leave the objects in a garage or outhouse at first and then gradually introduce them into the new home.

To help arthriticky pets with stiff or aching joints, the thoughtful owner will provide raised food and water bowls. This is most easily done by placing the vessels on a block of wood.

BRINGING YOUR DOG HOME

It may be wise to give the dog tranquillizers, such as acepromazine or diazepam (Valium), obtained from the vet, if the journey to your home is a long one. Such medication can also be useful in some cases when given at night for the first few days after arrival to particularly nervous or unsettled animals.

When the dog enters your home, he should be treated gently but not over-fussed, particularly by children of whom he may have little or no experience. Give him a meal, then commence the toilet regime by taking him outside to let him relieve himself. If the newcomer is a puppy this still applies, unless you have installed a litter tray. (The problem with litter trays is that those dogs that bury their faeces tend to do it quite vigorously and can kick litter over a large area. Later on, this can encourage dogs to use flower beds as toilets rather than lawns or solid surfaces.)

Arrange for your dog's bed to be located in some quiet, draught-free, snug area outside the main traffic routes through the house.

CHECKLIST FOR RESCUE DOGS

1   Is the dog physically suitable for you? Consider its size, breed type, exercise requirements and coat type (long hair means regular grooming).

2   Is your situation suitable for the dog? Do you have enough available space, opportunities for exercise, accessibility to walks and parks, other pets in the household, any restrictions on pet ownership in your home or apartment block, any disabilities or allergies in family members that might affect owning and caring for a dog? How long might the dog be left alone in the house and where?

3   Can you afford the 'running costs' of the dog – feeding, health care, boarding fees, grooming, etc? This is particularly pertinent to older dogs with health problems.

4   How does the dog look to you? Friendly, wary, aggressive, etc? Does it seem to have normal physical proportions and to be able to move normally? Are there any obvious physical deformities or abnormalities that you should ask about? If visible, do its stools appear formed and normal?

5   How long has it been in the dog's home? Has it been adopted previously and, if so, how many times, for how long and why was it returned?

6   Are there any papers (pedigree, vaccination certificates, veterinary reports, etc.) with it? Make sure you ask to see these before taking the dog home.

7   Has the attending vet examined it? What is his or her opinion of the dog? Roughly what age is it: young, middle-aged or old? Is it on any medication?

8   If a bitch, has she been spayed? If not, is she possibly pregnant? Find out whether she has had puppies as this could affect her behaviour.

9   What is its diet? Is it known to be allergic to anything? Once you know what the breed is, find out the recommended diet as well as quantities to feed it.

10 Have you had enough, or indeed any, experience in looking after this kind of pet? A dog is a responsibility for everyone in the household to take a share of.

Dogs and babies

Introducing a new dog to a baby is a process that demands considerable care and preparation. Dogs see children as human members of the family pack and, indeed, can be very protective of them in the presence of strangers. Such desirable protectiveness is actually far commoner than signs of jealousy. Babies, however, are a different matter. They may not be 'recognized' as human. They don't move about and generally 'behave' like humans, and they make unusual noises. On the other hand, the dog knows they are clearly not dogs, so could they be some other form of animal, in particular a prey animal? Certain dogs seem to imagine so on occasion, and with them there is a risk of predatory aggression towards the infant.

If at all possible bring some of the new arrival's familiar things, particularly its bed, from its old home.

Dogs must never be left alone with infants under any circumstances. The biggest risk is from dogs with a known history of aggression towards people, but even the most amiable and unaggressive pet can inadvertently injure a baby by jumping up, pawing at or nudging it.

How should you handle this? Control through basic obedience training is vital. Preventing access to a room where the baby is alone is essential. If in any doubt, the dog should wear a soft muzzle. Prior to the birth, owners can accustom their pet to having a baby around by regularly 'play-acting' with a doll, nursing it, dressing and undressing it, tucking it into bedding and so forth.

Before the baby first comes home from hospital with its mother, it is useful for other family members to bring back blankets or nappies bearing the baby's smell for the dog to become acquainted with. When mother and baby do eventually arrive, the first meeting with the dog should be without the presence of the baby. A little later the baby can be brought in, carried by another family member.

Over the next few days the dog, on a halter and lead, can be introduced to the infant, at first from a distance and then gradually closer and closer. On each occasion, good behaviour and calmness on the part of the dog should be rewarded with praise and a food treat. He must at all times receive no less attention than he is used to.

Meeting other pets

Introductions to any other pets should be made cautiously and always under your full supervision. Older, more aggressive canine residents, especially dogs rather than bitches, can resent the presence of a new animal while, on the other hand, a newcomer with a domineering nature may in some cases immediately challenge the incumbent animal. Generally, however, the longer a dog has lived in a household the more authority and status he has.

Watch the animals carefully for at least a week, and be even-handed in giving praise and in patting or stroking them. Keep their feeding places well separated and organize socializing in which you play a full part acting as pack leader. Going out for walks on the lead together is preferable at first to games with balls where the dogs may compete and end up quarrelling over matters of dominance.

Introducing your new pet to the existing dog or bitch in the household is best done outside on neutral territory. It is best to have one or two dog-friendly adults around in case things get out of hand. Very young children should not be involved at this stage. A park or other open space where you do not regularly walk your current pet is best, as your dog will not have any 'territorial' feelings towards it. Both animals should be on long, ideally retractable 'flexi' leads, which allow them to be easily controlled. Once the dogs get along reasonably well in the park, you can try them together at home, but only after temporarily removing possible foci of jealous confrontation such as the incumbent pet's bed and favourite toys.

Cats usually resent the intrusion of a new pet in the house, particularly a dog. They will tend to make themselves scarce for the first few weeks until they begin, often under protest, to accept the idea. The control of the situation by you, the pack leader, when the dog and cat are in the same room is critical. If the dog lunges at the cat your response must be to prevent any contact occuring and talk soothingly to one or other of the protagonists,

The new arrival should be kept on a lead when meeting other pets in the household.

whichever is most appropriate, but never to punish. If you clip a dog's ear when he makes for Puss he will come to resent the cat as the cause of the cuffing – and perhaps wait to seek revenge when you are not around.

This piece of advice may seem to run counter to what we discuss concerning dogs connecting two pieces of information occurring closely in time (see page 38), and also to Pavlovian principles. Indeed, it is the exception that proves the rule, for in many cases the idea of vengeance for perceived indignities changes the subsequent behaviour of the dog, although it is unlikely to be enduring. Dogs don't normally bear a grudge against the family cat for long. It is not usually necessary to keep a dog and cat apart when no one is in the house. Cats can almost always find some safe haven under furniture or on top of a shelf out of canine reach wherein to drowse away the day.

Dog and cat introductions can be handled by the owner by first tying the dog's lead to some fixed point in a room with sufficient escape routes and high surfaces to give the cat confidence in its own safety. The cat is then brought in and the owner stands by, observing. If the dog lunges at the cat, it is ignored and given no eye contact. Then, when the dog responds to the owner calling it by name, and obeys commands to come and sit, it is rewarded by food titbits and fulsome praise and fuss. The dog will soon learn that, while it gets nothing but the owner's cold shoulder for having a go at the cat, it is well rewarded when it behaves politely in the cat's presence.

Routines and training

From the beginning, you must establish routines of feeding, toilet time and exercise, and initiate or reinforce obedience training in the new environment. Regular exercise is essential. A recent survey has shown

Begin training and setting routines as soon as possible after arrival, including rewarding good behaviour.

that one in four people in the UK are too busy and stressed-out to walk their pets every day. As a consequence, the dogs themselves frequently begin to suffer from stress! Save all rewards for use in training – they have to be earned. Particularly with young animals, never give rewards that are simply begged for by, for example, pawing, nudging or barking.

Correct undesirable behaviour, including displays of dominance or 'pushiness' as soon as it occurs (see page 92). Handle all the animals (established and newly introduced) frequently, and always reward obedience and a correct response to any command. Don't permit rough, boisterous play, such as tug of war, unless you initiate it.

Handling, stroking and, particularly, grooming your new dog should be performed by all family members, and he must be taught to accept any approach or handling by a human being when he is feeding or playing with a toy without showing resentment or aggression. If he is inclined to react badly in these circumstances, then you must begin training to gradually wean him away from the unwanted response. Whatever it is that triggers the response should be performed in a most gentle manner accompanied by quiet praise and a food reward. The length and intensity of these 'desensitizing' training sessions, given to the dog on a regular daily basis, should gradually be increased (see chapter 7).

Of course, all this revolves around you acting as pack leader. The dog arriving in your household is being introduced into a new pack, and he must recognize that you are the dominant animal, the alpha individual, and let there be no misunderstanding of this from the start. All other human members of the household must be in a position of higher dominance than the dog, or dogs, and they also must apply the rules of handling, training and reinforcing training dealt with in this book, otherwise dogs may respect and obey some family members but not others, particularly children. It is especially important that everyone understands how to control, not punish, the dog. Children can easily drift into ideas of punishment for pets; they must not do this under any circumstances. Training or retraining for unwelcome behaviour must begin promptly as soon as the dog arrives in its new home.

The dog will look at you and your family and see a pack – of dogs. He will treat you all as members of a pack in which there is a hierarchy. He will find his niche in the hierarchy and, if things develop as they should, that niche will be at the bottom, with all human family pack members higher up. In due course, he will come to respect human leadership; this is vital if he is to be obedient and well behaved. Among wild dog and wolf packs, if a liberty-taking young dog is not disciplined and given leadership, it is likely to try climbing the hierarchical pyramid, even to the point of challenging the position of ultimate dominance held by the alpha dog.

The same process can take place in a family pack if you (alpha human) do not assert your dominance from the beginning and fail to insist on compliance from your dog in all aspects of his daily life, from feeding and exercise periods to settling down at night. Dogs must respect the more dominant position of all the family members, including children. The latter

TRACKING DEVICES

It is well worthwhile having the new arrival micro-chipped, if it has not been already. These tiny devices injected under the skin can be read electronically by readers that most vets, rescue homes, customs officers and other officials possess – allowing identification of a dog should it get lost as well as being essential as part of the pet passport procedure if taking the animal abroad.

sometimes do not understand this, but you must explain it carefully to them, especially the fact that firm control of your new pet must not be equated with punishment.

Undesirable behaviours

Your new dog may bring with him behavioural tendencies and bad habits, which were ignored or tolerated by his previous owner. But the very act of moving into your household – a new environment, a new family/pack group containing perhaps not only humans but also other animals, and a new daily routine – can trigger behavioural problems. And then there is the inexorable effect of ageing. As the dog enters canine senior citizenship, a variety of geriatric conditions may begin to affect him, some mental, some physical, and all of them can produce changes in behaviour. The main problem behaviours are:

- aggression
- excitability/unruliness, including running away
- excessive barking
- destructive behaviour
- excessive submission
- fears and phobias
- soiling and toilet problems
- compulsive and stereotypical behaviours
- eating droppings
- food and feeding-related problems.

I will deal with each of these and the ways to tackle them in the following chapters. Most types of undesirable behaviour are more frequently seen in younger animals, particularly excessive submission and unruliness which are seldom a problem in dogs over about seven years of age. In the experience of most animal behaviourists, at least three-quarters of cases of aggression towards people are exhibited by dogs under nine years old. One thing is certain: there are no problem dogs, only some dogs with problems.

A dog has the soul of a philosopher.
PLATO

BEHAVIOUR AND INTELLIGENCE

3

Before we go on to discuss training and, beyond that, the correction of undesirable behaviour in your pet, it is worth considering the intelligence, skills and attitude of the normal dog as well as learning to understand its body language.

CANINE INTELLIGENCE

The creation of a harmonious relationship between dog and owner depends on each learning to understand the other, and for this to happen, intelligence is required in both parties. Defining what we mean by intelligence and, even more so, comparing the intelligence of different species is not easy. It is difficult enough to compare that of humans conditioned by different cultures. With dogs, the question is even trickier – different breeds have developed a wide range of distinct physical abilities and natural instincts. Just think of the immediately apparent differences between toy and giant breeds, guard breeds and sight hounds, fighting dogs and herding dogs.

Some modern scientists, echoing the opinions once voiced by the theologian Thomas Aquinas and, later, the French philosopher, Descartes, consider animals to be no more than 'mere machines', nervous systems that are simply bundles of electrical wiring controlling a body of muscle and other tissues purely by instinctive response to the world around them, void of emotion, feeling or true consciousness. Others, among whom I include myself, take a different view similar to that of Aristotle in classical times, that humans and dogs differ in their possession of mental abilities only by degree. Both have emotion; it is simply that the range of human emotions is more complex and elaborate. Dogs learn, remember, benefit from experience and solve problems. So do humans, only far better. Some folk take it even farther and argue that if animals are intelligent and human beings have evolved from animals, dogs could have souls, albeit souls not as highly developed as ours, but let's leave that to the philosophers and theologians.

How dogs perceive the world

It is certainly true that one of the biggest stumbling blocks in setting up intelligence tests for dogs is the fact that they perceive the world quite differently to humans and have different ways of processing the information received by their brains concerning that world. For instance, dogs do not see colour to any degree, seemingly not much more than some blue and yellow, and certainly colour is of little relevance to them. Nor do they have much appreciation of visual detail, an ability that is highly developed in humans. The canine world is much more boldly depicted in scent than ours, and their brains contain bigger areas concerned with processing motion and scent data than those of humans.

'Human' behaviour

Though significantly bigger than that of its ancestors in the days when creodonts were around, the dog's brain is much smaller than man's. Like their wolf relatives they have a large neocortex, an area involved in reasoning, in the brain The ability to think certainly isn't absent but is much reduced, although dogs do occasionally give the impression of working things out mentally and behaving in a surprisingly 'human' way. A famous canine example is Greyfriars Bobby, a Skye Terrier who, after his master's death, followed the coffin to the churchyard and defied all efforts to shoo him away. The dog spent the next 14 years until his own death living around the churchyard apparently grieving for his lost friend and master.

Then there was Old Shep who maintained a five-year vigil at the railway in Fort Benton, Montana, after seeing the coffin of his master loaded onto a train, and every April eighth when Japanese dog lovers pay homage at the Shibuya underground station in Tokyo to Hachiko, an Akita, one of the three breeds native to Japan, and another remarkably faithful canine. Hachiko belonged to a Tokyo university don, Professor Ueno. Each day the dog would walk to the station to welcome his master as he came back from work. After the professor died in 1925, Hachiko continued to meet the train every single day until he himself died in 1934.

Comparative intelligence

Scientists have approached the question of comparative intelligence in two ways. One, the better of the two in my view, is to calculate the amount of brain tissue which is more than that needed to control the basic functions of the body – breathing, circulating the blood, moving etc. This 'excess' brain capacity can be used by the animal to gain more information via its senses about the world around it and to go on from there to construct perceptual models of that world; to put it

Highly sociable African hunting dogs recognize one another by means of their striking coat markings.

another way, to 'think' about life, to be 'intelligent'. As you might expect, humans, dolphins and chimpanzees come out top, while reptiles do badly and hedgehogs seem to be among the least intelligent of mammals. Deer, wolves, lemurs, dogs – and crows! – have similar, fairly high intelligence ratings, with dogs, blessed with more extensive smelling areas of the brain and greater development of their frontal lobes as a result of their complex social systems, calculated to be, on average, 38 per cent more intelligent than the mainly solitary-living cats, even though the latter have more development of the hearing areas in their brains. Dogs are also more intelligent than budgerigars and, I hate to say it to you Pony Club devotees, ponies.

The second method of evaluating comparative intelligence is the so-called ecological approach and is much easier to apply to wild animals than domestic ones.

ABILITY TO COUNT

For the wolves and dogs, pack-living animals, the ability to count would seem a useful ability both within the pack and when out hunting (noting the number of allies and enemies in a gathering, calculating the number of potential prey) and it does seem that these animals do indeed have a concept of numbers and can even do simple mathematical calculations. I am not referring to those performing dogs in variety shows and circuses that are apparently highly numerate; in almost all cases trickery of some sort is involved. The dog taps the bell when a certain number has been reached, for example, by responding to some sort of inconspicuous visual signal given by the handler and which the audience cannot see.

Recently, experiments similar to those employed to show that five-month-old babies can count, have been applied to dogs. A number of toy dolls are placed in front of a baby and then a screen is raised to hide them from its view. The baby watches as a number of dolls are added or taken, the experimenter's hand dipping behind the screen. Then the screen is removed. If the experimenter has surreptitiously added or taken away a doll and the numbers don't add up for it, the baby stares at the dolls for much longer than it does if the number of dolls is 'right'. Presumably it has done its calculations taking into account the experimenter's apparent additions or subtractions, but the resultant number of dolls contradicts its expectations.

When this experiment was done using 11 mongrel dogs and doggie treats instead of dolls the animals reacted in the same way, staring at the bowl of treats for much longer if their sums did not add up. The dogs seemed unconcerned when one treat plus one treat came to the expected total of two treats, but when one treat plus one treat apparently equalled three they were clearly confused. It is thought that dogs, like many mammals, may be able to count as high as seven.

It defines intelligence in the ability to deal with sudden changes in their situation by using new patterns of behaviour to deal with the unfamiliar circumstances. It is the ability to conceptualize, to extrapolate from one situation to another. How though to quantify this type of ability in your dog? It is exceedingly difficult. All I can say is that dogs almost certainly have more complex minds than comparative psychologists have yet been able to measure.

Forms of canine intelligence

A Canadian professor of experimental psychology who is also a dog trainer, Stanley Coren, has investigated the dog's mind and claims in his book, *The Intelligence of Dogs* (The Free Press, 1994), to have identified three separate forms:

1 ADAPTIVE INTELLIGENCE: learning ability and problem solving. This enables an individual to adapt to their environment, even perhaps modify it, by quickly assembling incoming pieces of information, processing them, applying them to any new situation and storing the solution to the problem in the memory bank.

2 WORKING OR OBEDIENCE INTELLIGENCE: the ability to respond appropriately to various commands. Here a dog must be able to concentrate, possessing a long attention span that is not easily distracted. It must also respond quickly when its handler communicates with it in some manner and it should show mental flexibility in trying another approach if its first responses to a command are not rewarded.

3 INSTINCTIVE INTELLIGENCE: genetically determined abilities and behavioural predispositions that allow a dog to do a particular job well – for example, terriers to go underground, spaniels to flush game birds, or border collies to herd sheep.

When we speak of canine intelligence, Professor Coren would argue that a mix of all three of the above types of intelligence is involved in any one individual animal. One obvious difficulty in testing dogs' intelligence is the fact that the various breeds were bred to be, and are, specialists in certain ways. How then to set up tests that are fair to all?

Sight hounds, such as Greyhounds, would clearly perform better in tests involving visual clues than scent hounds – and vice versa. Similarly, the good hunting Beagle displays 'intelligence' when out at work that would not be appropriate in, say, a Border Collie. The Beagle concentrates intently on picking up and then following a scent trail to its source. It will ignore all distractions apart from the commands of its owner. By contrast, a Border Collie working a flock of sheep must be able to juggle multiple incoming perceptions simultaneously, including distractions. It must keep the sheep moving towards the goal, not too fast, not too slow. It must keep an eye out for stragglers, dawdlers or fugitives. And it must observe the area around the flock for any sign of danger or difficulty, all the while with an ear cocked and the occasional quick glance, alert to respond to any signal from the shepherd. And what about the good old mongrel? All of us have met the patently highly intelligent mongrel mutt at some time or other. How to compare him to a Borzoi or an Australian cattle dog? Impossible.

Coren's research is highly contentious, but he has come up with a list – in his view, not mine – of the most intelligent and least intelligent dog breeds. They are:

- THE BRIGHTEST BREEDS: Border Collie, Poodle, German Shepherd, Golden Retriever, Dobermann Pinscher, Shetland Sheepdog, Labrador Retriever, Papillon, Rottweiler. The Border Collie is claimed to be the most intelligent.
- THE LEAST BRIGHT BREEDS: Shih-Tzu, Basset Hound, Mastiff, Beagle, Pekingese, Bloodhound, Borzoi, Chow, Bulldog, Basenji, Afghan Hound. The Afghan Hound is claimed to be the dimmest.

I can only say that, as a veterinary surgeon for nearly 50 years, I have met some needle-sharp Afghans, Bassets and Shih-Tzus.

ASSOCIATION SKILLS

We know that dogs are capable of linking two ideas in their mind. The Russian scientist, Pavlov, famously demonstrated the ability of dogs to associate the sound of a ringing bell with feeding time. They cannot, however, associate events, that are separated in time. If your dog goes AWOL while you are out on a walk, punishing him on his eventual return, two hours later, will not have the desired effect. He will think the punishment is the reward for returning; he cannot comprehend that punishment was for something he did hours ago. The correct approach is to make returning a pleasurable experience for him; give him kind words, a friendly pat and a favourite treat. The idea is to make the dog want to come back to please you! It is the secret of all good training.

Make sure that coming home is as much fun as going out for a walk. Playing a game is just as much reward for a dog's good behaviour as a food treat.

FRONTAL LOBES

Though significantly bigger than that of its ancestors in the days of creodonts the dog's brain is much smaller than man's. Whereas a human brain weighs about one-fortieth of the total body weight, a dog's weighs a one-hundred-and-twenty-fifth. The frontal lobes of dogs begin to shrink before the rest of the brain with approaching old age, usually at somewhere between eight and eleven years when the first signs of senile behaviour changes may appear. The frontal lobes are involved in many of the brain's fundamental functions, including motor function, problem solving, memory, judgement, initiation and social and sexual behaviour. In humans, they are also the seat of personality, emotional control and creation of language. The more frontal lobe an animal possesses – man, the great apes and the dolphins are the leaders in this field – the more intelligent it is. The trouble is, however, in defining what we mean by 'intelligence'.

Communicating with your dog

Your dog's 'desire to please' characteristic has to be linked to communication with you, his owner, in some way for training to be successful. Dogs are superb at detecting subtle signals from humans, whether these are unconscious signals of pleasure, distress or anger, or simply the intention to do something. They look at us just as the individuals in a pack of wild dogs look at their fellows, interacting via visible body language and sounds to express emotions. They don't understand our speech but rather the pattern and tone of the words. Sound signals are just as eloquent given by a whistle, whether achieved by sticking two fingers in your mouth or using the teacher's metal device, provided the dog has been taught to recognise the whistle as a signal akin to a verbal command, as is the case with sheepdogs.

An inexpensive whistle can provide an extra means of communicating with your dog.

This excellent ability to appreciate visual and audible signals, often quite low-key, unobtrusive ones, is used at a sophisticated level by professional trainers putting together dog acts for films, television and circuses. Dogs are not trained by fear but by the wish to please. This can motivate them to learn complex manoeuvres to be carried out in response to signals, even at long range. I frequently supervise such animals when they are working on film sets and have never seen a single case of a dog being punished. They patently enjoy 'treading the boards' and are clearly concerned only with impressing their trainers who, of course, always have their pockets stuffed with goodies.

CANINE INSTINCTS

As a result of man's artificial selection, producing breeds that were used for a particular purpose, modern dogs possess innate traits which do not require special training. For instance, retrievers love to pick up objects in their mouth and carry them around with obvious great pride. Pointers 'point' unconsciously at things that interest them before investigating further. Sheepdogs just love herding all animals, including people. The Dobermann, Spitz-type animals and terriers are all instinctive guards.

Hunting and chasing instincts

Like their wild relatives, domestic dogs are predatory carnivores. Even though well fed by you, some will still instinctively go through the motions of hunting and catching prey. They may stalk, catch and even kill small animals, but often an impressive-looking dash at the target creature is aborted at the last moment. It's just the 'thrill of the chase'.

Cats, of course, are great sport for many dogs. It's not that even a hungry dog would consider them edible, but being small, furry, quick in movement and inclined to run away, they appeal to the ancient hunting urge deep in the canine soul. Again, usually the chase is harmless, ending when the irate cat turns and adopts a defensive posture, hissing and spitting ferociously. Dogs distinguish between cats and will happily coexist with their own family cat, even allowing the latter to take impertinent liberties, while still chasing the cat next door when it hoves into view.

Another animal that, by turning tail and running from a dog, acts as natural prey is the sheep. Dogs unaccustomed to sheep will often chase them. Sheep worrying is a serious matter from time to time for some farmers.

Retrievers love retrieving and they're not fussy what it is! This characteristic is in their genes.

Although a marauding dog or dogs (not infrequently, rather like human yobs when the pubs close, a group of them will go out looking to make mischief) may merely engage in herding manoeuvres, giving up when the sheep are huddled together in a corner of a field, they do sometimes bite and even kill. Even without biting, canine harassment can cause serious injury to pregnant ewes and lambs. It is not surprising that shepherds may well shoot a dog seen worrying sheep. When walking your pet near sheep, don't take any risks; keep him to heel on a lead.

Digging instincts

Another instinctive behaviour that is seen in dogs is digging. Their early ancestors would store food in the ground to help them survive the leaner hunting days. Jackals commonly cache left-over food in this way, usually returning within 24 hours to exhume it when hungry again. Some pet dogs do bury bones and

THE DOG'S PACK

The dog regards humans as well as other dogs as its own kind while often ignoring birds and other creatures. Its pack is the family. The family home is the pack's territory. Unknown human or canine individuals are viewed with initial suspicion as being from outside the pack. The dog's owner is regarded as leader of the pack, literally 'top dog'. If a stranger (human or dog) is accepted without aggression by the pack leader, he, she or it will normally be accepted by the dog: 'If it's OK with da boss, it's OK by me.' In the absence of the pack leader, the dog understandably, steps in and takes over the role. Even a small, normally unassuming bitch under these circumstances may show a surprising degree of territorial aggression: 'Da boss is out. Come back later! So beat it!'

The classic example, of course, is the dog's attitude to the postman. Look at it from the canine point of view: up the path comes Postman Pat. The leader of the pack does not come out to greet him. The dog warns the postman off by barking. Guess what, the postman turns tail after doing some fumbling for a few seconds at the door but failing to enter. The dog is triumphant! He has driven off this stranger who clearly is a rank coward. It only took a bark or two and the fellow was off! Each day dog and intruder go through the same motions. The dog recognizes sooner or later that uniform is the mark of a coward who can be chased and who can be expected to retreat literally post haste.

If you have this sort of a problem and the Post Office are threatening to cross you off the mail round, you should arrange to go out to greet the postman when he calls on a few consecutive mornings, and then less frequently but on a regular basis, so that your dog can see the pack leader chatting amicably and smiling with the suspicious character.

Dogs live in a world of smells that mere humans are incapable of visiting.

return later to dig them up with much enthusiasm. It is a pity this fondness for digging cannot be harnessed to the point where dogs might do my gardening for me, supervised of course, gin and tonic in hand, from my deck-chair!

Scenting instincts

Smell is supremely important to dogs. Sniffing anything unfamiliar – including other dogs and humans – is one of the dog's strongest instincts. Where we humans react primarily on the basis of sight and sound, dogs rely heavily on smell. The average dog's nose is about 10,000 to 100,000 times more sensitive than our own. It also has 40 times the number of brain cells involved in scent recognition than the number in the human. Part of the increased sensitivity of the dog's nose is due to it having a much larger sensory or olfactory area. In man this is about three square centimetres, but in the average dog it is 130 square centimetres. The sensory area is folded over many times, creating ridges which form a trapping mechanism for smells, and the sensory cells which pick up the odour chemicals are more closely packed together. The dog's relative, the wolf, has a nose so finely tuned that it can detect and analyse a three-week-old dried patch of urine from a distance of 300 metres. Domestic dogs can pick up the scent of a chemical at a dilution of one to two parts in a trillion, the equivalent of locating one bad apple in 2 billion barrels!

The importance of smell is shown by the male dog's (or wolf's) desire to urinate frequently – bitches do it too, but not so noticeably. The urine leaves an enduring scent marking what the dog considers to be, or is trying to claim as, his own territory. Similarly, a dog uses the strong-smelling secretion from the sebaceous glands in its anal sacs to put his own personal smell on his faeces. The reason a dog urinates so often is that he is competing with all other dogs in the scent stakes and trying to mask their scent. Humans often try to compete by talking loudest in company; dogs do it by peeing.

Another form of scent marking is scratching the ground with the hind paw, kicking up the earth. This leaves behind the scent produced by sweat glands in the hind paws. Sometimes dogs apply their own version of 'after-shave' by rolling in strong-smelling substances to reinforce their own smell. These usually smell terrible to us but enchanting to the dog – top favourites include pig manure and bird droppings.

BODY LANGUAGE

As they are not able to use speech to express feelings of uncertainty, aggression, fear, pleasure or playfulness, dogs instead use visible body signals to convey these emotions to other members of the pack or to strangers. It is very important that you, as your pet's fellow pack member, are able to recognize them. The signs are shown by the posture of the whole body and/or the expressions of the face. Barks, growls or whimpers give additional clues as to how the dog is feeling. You must be alert to and able to interpret signs based on body posture, vocalization (sounds), ears, eyes, lips, tongue, tail and hair (standing on end or not).

In a very real sense, the dog is 'talking' by means of these visual signs and signals. You, who must be able to communicate with him, as you would with another person whom you were instructing in some way, need to understand canine 'body language' if you are to successfully train and in any way modify your pet's behaviour. You use words and sounds as well as visual signals in training; the dog uses sounds and visual signals but no words. Even so, the communication between you is a two-way process.

Vocalization

Most dogs are fairly vocal, emitting a repertoire of sounds, ranging from whimpers through growls of varying intensity to barks. They use their voice to 'speak', to express themselves and raise the pitch or volume of their barks to indicate frustration or emotion. Barking is not necessarily aggressive; it more often means 'Hurry up, I'm ready to play!' or 'Nice to see you, how are you doing?' rather than 'One false move and I'll chew your leg off!' Researchers at the University of California recently studied the vocalizations of 10 dogs from six breeds and found that their barks varied according to the situation. For example, a high-pitched bark seemed to say 'Where is my owner?', while a lower-pitched, harsher one meant 'A stranger is coming!'

Growling is more often aggressive in adult dogs than puppies. Some dogs 'play growl' where a mock growl is produced when they are 'teasing', but as there are no other warning signs of body posture or facial expression, their mood is clearly non-aggressive. Again, a rolling sound, rather like a growl but fluctuating in pitch, can be considered non-aggressive. Aggressive growls have either a constant or steadily rising pitch and are accompanied by an aggressive body posture.

Body posture

The prospect of rewards is another way of initiating communication of sorts and in fact can lead to some dogs literally becoming actors. Having been fussed over and given food treats when slightly injured, or out of sorts on previous occasions, can result in these canine thespians faking the limp, or turning their head to one side (as they did when ear infection struck). The hope is to attract sympathy again and, more importantly, the titbit. Aside from these instances, it is usually fairly easy to read your dog's body 'language' and the moods and messages that he or she wants to convey are signified by a range of different body postures that, once learnt, will be invaluable in understanding your dog.

HAPPY/ CONTENT

A happy, alert dog carries his tail well with no tension in the body. He moves fluidly and holds his head high. The tongue may loll out of the mouth and the jaws are relaxed.

ASKING TO PLAY

When craving a game, a dog frequently dips down the front of his body into a crouch. He may raise one foot and lean to one side, his head almost touching the ground. He may jump backwards and forwards, the head looking up at you with relaxed jaws. Meanwhile, he is giving little yips and barks or high-pitched rolling growls.

The posture is unmistakeable: 'Come on, let's play!'.

SUBMISSION

The 'asking to play' posture may quickly pass into a submissive posture with the dog in a lower crouch. The front feet are usually raised one at a time in mild play invitation. The teeth cannot be seen. In this tension-free posture, the dog is probably silent. He may crouch even lower and lick a little. Some submissive dogs turn side-on to present a flank.

Abject submission: surrender could not be more obvious!

ABJECT SUBMISSION

Here the dog folds down his ears, and drops his
tail folding it around one leg or, if very nervous, tucking it right under the body. The head is down, eye contact being avoided, but with reassurance it comes up. The final stage in submission is rolling over, one hind leg raised. Unless afraid, the dog will usually raise his ears a little to show the submission stems from trust.

DOMINANT AGGRESSION

A dog in this mood advances confidently with both ears and tail held high. The teeth are bared, generally snapping and ready to bite. The dog looks straight at you or the canine opponent, intent and unblinking.

FEARFUL AGGRESSION

Here the dog shows his teeth,
utters a constant low
growl or snarl, or
even barks. The ears
are laid back with the
whole body tense and
the hind legs braced
ready for rapid movement.
The tail is held down and rigid
while the hair down the centre line
of his back stands on end.

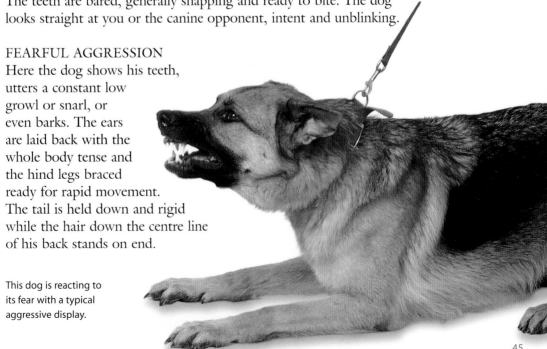

This dog is reacting to its fear with a typical aggressive display.

Facial expressions

We humans have the most expressive faces in the animal kingdom thanks to hundreds of small muscles that can quickly act in concert to shape our features into a multitude of expressions, sometimes subtle, sometimes dramatic. Dogs do not have such a sophisticated ability but they do possess facial muscles capable of giving a fairly limited range of expressions.

LIPS AND TEETH

The lips can be curled back to expose the teeth in the manner of a medieval gaoler showing the instruments of torture to his victim. Baring the dentures in this way is not always aggressive – some dogs seem almost to laugh and, when very pleased, their lips are drawn back further, exposing the pointed canine teeth or fangs.

An aggressive display of the dog's weaponry may well deter an opponent.

EARS

The highly mobile ears can turn to follow sounds. Even drop-eared dogs like spaniels can move their ears into an alert position, although they don't have the range of expression of those breeds with pricked ears.

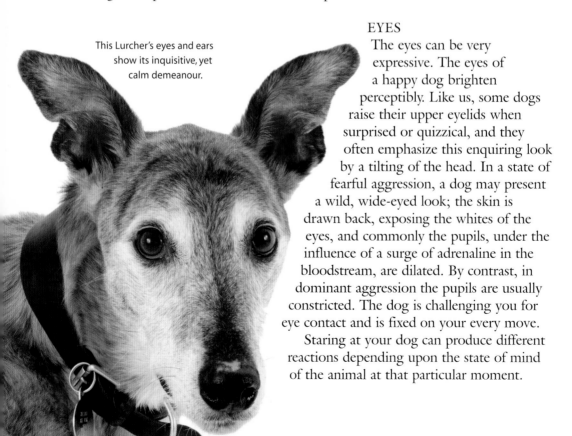

This Lurcher's eyes and ears show its inquisitive, yet calm demeanour.

EYES

The eyes can be very expressive. The eyes of a happy dog brighten perceptibly. Like us, some dogs raise their upper eyelids when surprised or quizzical, and they often emphasize this enquiring look by a tilting of the head. In a state of fearful aggression, a dog may present a wild, wide-eyed look; the skin is drawn back, exposing the whites of the eyes, and commonly the pupils, under the influence of a surge of adrenaline in the bloodstream, are dilated. By contrast, in dominant aggression the pupils are usually constricted. The dog is challenging you for eye contact and is fixed on your every move.

Staring at your dog can produce different reactions depending upon the state of mind of the animal at that particular moment.

Normally, staring at him will cause him to look away and become submissive, but if he is in a confident mood and knows and trusts you well, he may merely react with a questioning look. But beware. Do not try to 'stare out' a dog that you do not know unless you are confident of coping with the potential attack that may follow should you be first to break the eye-to-eye contact.

YAWNING

Yawning by a dog is not, as in humans, a sign of tiredness or boredom. It is rather a somewhat placatory gesture, usually on the part of a more dominant individual to a lesser that signifies: 'Don't worry, I mean you no harm.'
It can indicate uneasiness or anxiety too.

Tail talk

The tail is an important part of the dog's anatomy. Docking, done in almost all cases other than where there is a medical indication, purely for man's ideas of canine beauty, is an inexcusable mutilation. Apart from its use as a tool – water dogs use it as a rudder when swimming, for example – the tail is an important part of the animal's communication apparatus. Wagging it is a display of pleasure, holding it out straight from the body can indicate an aggressive attitude, tucking it under shows submission and fear.

Not a sign of boredom, yawning in dogs is more of a placatory gesture to a superior.

Professor Coren (see page 37) has investigated the 'language' of the dog's tail in great detail and claims to recognise the meaning of subtle differences in the tail's position or movement. Examples he gives are as follows:

- A broad tail wag means: *'I like you.'*
- A slight tail wag means: *'I see you looking at me. You like me, don't you?'*
- A slow tail wag with the tail at half-mast means: *'I want to know what you mean, but I just can't figure it out.'*
- A tail held almost horizontal, pointing away from the body but not stiff, is saying: *'Something interesting may be happening here.'*
- A tail held up and slightly curved over the back is declaring: *'I am top dog!'*
- A tail that is down near the hind legs with the legs bent slightly inwards is indicating: *'I'm feeling a bit insecure.'*

One of the undesirable results of docking is that the docked dog cannot easily signal submission and so may end up in an unwanted fight. It has been suggested that the original reason for docking breeds like Rottweilers and Dobermanns was exactly that: to stimulate aggression by preventing adequate expression of submission.

An old dog will learn no new tricks.

THOMAS D'URFEY, QUIXOTE

TRAINING YOUR DOG

4

We hear much nowadays about dogs, particularly spaniels, being trained to detect explosives, weapons, drugs, bodies and so forth. Incredibly, they can detect the smell trace left by human fingerprints on glass for up to six weeks if indoors, and two weeks if outdoors. They will follow the trail of a person even if he or she pauses to put on rubber boots or mounts a bicycle! But, even with their incredible innate sense of smell, they must receive months of exhaustive training before they go to work with the police, security services, etc. Quite recently dogs have even been trained to detect the presence of bladder cancer in human patients by sniffing their urine.

GOOD, EFFECTIVE TRAINING

Some years ago an incredibly clever advertisement for British Gas appeared on television. Picture a glowing gas fire in a living room. Into frame walks a dog who turns towards the warmth and sits down, with his back to camera. A moment later a cat does exactly the same, walking in and sitting next to the dog. Then a mouse scuttles into view and sits beside the cat. All three animals are now in a perfect row no more than millimetres apart and basking in the fire's glow. Jim Clubb, of Amazing Animals, one of the best humane animal trainers in Great Britain, organised the shoot which, on the day, incredibly, was accomplished in one take!

Training to those levels takes skill and man/animal understanding of the highest order. I am not expecting you to try anything so advanced in getting your new dog to do what you want, but good canine behaviour depends on good training by the owner. It has been suggested that bad behaviour by a dog has actually affected the course of history. When King Henry VIII wanted the Pope to annul his marriage to Catherine of Aragon he sent Cardinal Wolsey to the Vatican to plead his case. Curiously, Wolsey took his pet Greyhound, Urian, with him to Rome. When Wolsey, still accompanied by Urian, was shown into the papal presence he knelt in obeisance to kiss the Pope's toe. At that moment the Greyhound shot forward and clamped his jaws on the Pope's foot. That bite put an end to the negotiations; Henry wasn't granted a divorce and presently opted to found the Church of England. I think it can thus be fairly stated that a badly behaved dog was the cause of the English Reformation!

HOW TO COMMUNICATE

Dog training is, in essence, the communication of a command, by sight or sound, to the animal instructing it to

---

BEST FOR **TRAINING**

THE MOST EASILY TRAINED BREEDS: Retrievers, German Shepherd, Dobermann, Rottweiler, Poodle, Sheltie, Corgi, Border Collie.
NOT SO EASILY TRAINABLE BREEDS: Husky, Boxer, Pekingese, Chow, Afghan Hound, Yorkshire Terrier, Cavalier King Charles Spaniel, Irish Setter, Cocker Spaniel, Hounds, Bulldog.
NOTE: Obviously there are individuals that are exceptions to the above

do something it understands and is stored in its memory bank. The relationship between handler and dog must be one of mutual respect, free of fear, with both parties attentive and employing an unambiguous common 'language'. Many experienced dog trainers believe clever dogs to be more difficult to train than, how shall I put it, the somewhat dimmer ones. The reason for this is probably because the sharper animals differentiate carefully between the various words they hear from their handler. It is as if they have a broader and more precise knowledge of the human vocabulary. Clever dogs can be considered to be rather pedantic. The same applies to visual signals; they must be clear and consistent time after time.

Sloppy talk or careless hand signals, (indeed any imprecision or ambiguity on our part), make it difficult for an animal to respond correctly. A dog trainer has to be consistent in his or her use of voice or visual commands. (This applies even more to those super-intelligent animals, dolphins and whales, with which I spend much of my working time. A presenter in a dolphin show who is inconsistent, slow or imprecise in his signals will cause irritation, boredom, and impatience in Flipper who, if he could speak English, would surely say: 'Oh, for goodness sake, come on! Decide what you want me to do or I'm off!') And with poorly skilled handlers the dolphins do often swim off to do their own thing.

Take the case of an inexperienced boy handling his dog at an obedience class, as described by Professor Coren. At one point the boy commanded his very bright Golden Retriever, Shadow, by using the words, 'Come on, Shadow, sit down!' Perfectly understandable syntax to us, but confusing, clumsy language to the dog which, after a moment of uncertainty, lowered his body to the ground and then began with his front paws to drag himself very awkwardly, and whimpering as he went, towards the boy. Shadow had understood that his handler was telling him to do two things at one and the same time. He wasn't happy, but gave it his best shot.

I remember a similar case where a lady training her Whippet was wont to command 'Silver, come and sit!', repeating the words two or three times. The confusion in the dog's mind was plainly evident. He looked hesitant and on edge. Should he go to his mistress or sit where he was. I watched him compromise by hesitantly walking halfway towards her very slowly with eyes pleading for clarification and then sitting down – no tail wagging there. The instructor at the obedience class had great difficulty in explaining the problem to the lady and the Whippet was confused time and again over several weeks' classes until finally the penny dropped in the owner's mind although she continued to opine to other dog owners that 'Silver is a bit slow, you know.'

BENEFITS OF TRAINING

A trained dog is more fun to have around, lives a safer life and, dog psychologists tell us, is a happier animal. Of course, some dogs train better and more easily than others and this is particularly true of the old dog that moves to a new family who often do not know the voice commands and signals used by the previous owner, or if indeed he was trained at all. Some dogs may have difficulty in certain training behaviours because of medical conditions, such as arthritis or incipient deafness, but as long as the handler appreciates the situation, then suitable new ways of teaching the pet can be employed. As with us humans, some canine individuals are quicker learners than others and the innate characteristics of a breed are important factors. A Pointer, for example, may not be quick to get the idea of walking on a lead; he has been bred to locate and indicate scent targets. He isn't a natural 'trot-along-at-his-master's-heel' sort of dog… but he will learn.

You may prefer to join an obedience class or let a professional dog trainer educate your new pet, but for most people do-it-yourself is the most rewarding and enjoyable way of training their newly arrived family dog. The essential behaviours of basic training are 'Walking to heel', 'Come', 'Sit', 'Stay/Wait' and 'Down'. The ingredients of training these and, later, more sophisticated behaviours are some form of command and reward or punishment depending upon correct response or otherwise.

TRAINING BY REWARD

This is the giving of 'presents' to the animal in appreciation of it having done the correct, desired thing. The reward can be a scrap of food, a favourite proprietary 'treat', a rub or pat of the head or body, a spot of playing together, a toy, going for a walk or even merely giving it some attention.

Suitable treats for dogs include dog biscuits, proprietary meat-based treats and pieces of cheese.

Positive reinforcement

The reward is only given as a so-called 'positive reinforcement' when the dog behaves correctly as instructed by you. If wrongly given in other circumstances it can act as a 'positive reinforcer' that encourages undesirable behaviour. For example, suppose you have a dog who is constantly jumping up at family members, pestering for attention. It may seem natural to pet the dog and say something like 'Oh stop it, Fido. You are a fusspot!' but the result is to stimulate repetition of the nuisance behaviour.

Negative reinforcement

This is the administering of a check or punishment that the dog dislikes and withdrawing it when the correct behaviour is performed. It is normally used in conjunction with 'positive reinforcement' and not as a standalone training tool.

Secondary reinforcement

A third form of reinforcement in training is 'secondary reinforcement'. This system was originally introduced in the 1960s for the humane training of dolphins in marine park displays and, more controversially, for undersea warfare. Dolphins cannot be trained by application of physical punishment – were it to be tried, they would simply swim off – but, sadly, dogs, elephants, horses, chimpanzees and many other mammalian species sometimes are subjected to it. Secondary reinforcement is particularly useful where it is not appropriate or possible to reward a behaviour at the proper time. The commonest form of 'secondary reinforcer' is the sound produced by a small hand-held clicker. The click tells the dog that it has performed correctly and that a

The clicker is an inexpensive device, which is very useful in training.

reward will be forthcoming. It bridges the gap between canine response and a reward from the owner. Other 'secondary reinforcers' that can be used are whistles, horns or even just a phrase like 'Good boy!' They can be introduced to the training programme by using them immediately and regularly after giving the reward – the 'primary reinforcer'. For training deaf dogs, a flash from a pen torch makes an excellent substitute for a click.

PUNISHMENT

Any kind of corporal punishment must *never* be used on a dog. Hitting, beating, kicking, pressing the lips down hard on its teeth – all of these are utterly taboo. There are some professional trainers who do employ physical punishment in training dogs, and you should have nothing to do with them. Apart from being plain cruel, hitting a dog can have various bad side effects. It increases fear of the owner and may lead to fear- or pain-induced aggression. Laboratory experiments have shown that physical punishment, when it appears to work, has no long-lasting effect unless it is of great intensity, perhaps at a level to inflict trauma. Clearly such measures are unethical.

Force is not a good training tool. Hitting a dog simply trains it to stay out of range, but training needs close contact and a good relationship so this counteracts your objective. There will be times, however, when you have to punish your dog – probably to stop him doing something wrong and to gain his attention. We have discussed the importance of praise as a positive reinforcement in training. With-holding that praise or he normal friendly pat on his head will act as a 'punishment' to the dog who is keen to please you.

If you need to go any further, think carefully about why you are using the punishment and be sure in your own mind that your dog will understand why he is being punished, and that he will link the punishment to the erroneous or disobedient act. Interrupt whatever he is doing wrong in a strong, sharp, even startling way. A loud, scolding 'No!' may suffice on its own. If not, the word can be reinforced with some harmless but unexpected use of an air horn, the rattle of a can, a puff from a citronella aerosol or a squirt from a water bottle. For some kinds of wrongful behaviour there are various devices on the market (see page 57). Whenever an undesirable behaviour has been interrupted and punished, make a point of going on to encourage a display of the correct behaviour, naturally with attendant rewards if all goes well.

CRATE TRAINING

Confining a dog, even an old one, in a cage or crate is sometimes recommended to prevent undesirable behaviours, such as house soiling and destructiveness. Many dog trainers, particularly in the United States, are well-disposed towards or indeed enthusiastic about this method of correction for certain behaviours, arguing that dogs, like their wolf forbears, are naturally 'den-orientated' animals. (In fact, members of the wolf and dog family, other than pregnant females, do not usually

1 Make sure the crate is suitably furnished, with toys, a water bowl and bedding and accustom your dog to being inside with the door open.

2 Once your dog is occupied, try closing the door, first for only a couple of minutes at a time.

seek out dens or hidey-holes.) Other behavioural experts regard crate or cage confinement as undesirable and ineffective. The words 'crate training' can perhaps evoke images of an animal imprisoned in something like a tea chest. I think the method is better entitled 'confinement training'.

If a crate, typically a travelling box, is to be used, it is essential that it should be big enough, i.e. at least 15 cm (6 in) longer than the length of the dog from the tip of its nose to the end of its horizontally stretched-out tail and with a floor area that is at least the square of that length. The crate should be sited in some quiet spot, ideally at the dog's preferred, regular sleeping

3 The crate can be semi-covered, for warmth, if the dog seems happy. The dog should enjoy going in.

place. It should be furnished with clean, comfortable bedding, a supply of drinking water and some of the dog's toys. A dog should not be confined in it longer than the normal night sleeping period and four to five hours during the day. Longer periods of confinement can create problems, such as frantic efforts to escape or the development of neuroses If being confined leads to any signs of anxiety such as constant whining, repetitive pacing or self-mutilation, the use of a crate must stop.

One preferable way of confining dogs, particularly puppies, is by means of a child's play pen. For bigger dogs, a dog-proofed room set aside for the purpose or a wire-meshed outside run, may be possible. These must also be furnished with comfortable bedding, a water supply and playthings to keep the dog happy.

OTHER TRAINING DEVICES

Some of these items are useful in tackling behavioural problems and will be mentioned later. I consider certain other devices to be inhumane and would advise against using them. Harmful devices include shock collars and choke collars.

Halter-collars and body harnesses

When training a dog to walk on a lead, a flat fabric collar is fine. Once trained, a harness or halter-collar can be used which is a combination of collar and muzzle used with a lead which exerts pressure over the nose and behind the ears that is far less forceful than when applied to a collar alone but more effective. However, care must be taken when using a halter-collar with short-nosed dogs, such as Boxers and Pugs, as, unless they are very carefully fitted, they can be harmful, sometimes damaging their nostrils or tear ducts. Although halter collars are fine for most

1 One size does NOT fit all. Buy the correct size halter-collar for your dog, then place over the muzzle first.

2 Fix it behind the dog's head, ensuring it is not loose and not too tight. It should be away from the eyes.

3 Clip the halter-collar to your dog's own flat collar. The lead then attaches to the flat collar as normal.

younger dogs, old timers with arthriticky necks or spines can also find them uncomfortable. For them, and all other dogs that pull, I recommend using a body harness. Body harnesses control the dog in a much safer and more humane way than the collar alone which can exert damaging pressure on the windpipe (trachea).

Remotely controlled collar devices

These are completely humane and are now becoming available. One emits a puff of citronella oil vapour; another vibrates (useful in training deaf dogs). Both of these can be used to interrupt an unwanted behaviour or as a 'secondary reinforcer' of good behaviour in the manner of a clicker. Obviously, to avoid confusion, these devices should be used for one purpose or another with any individual dog.

Ultra-sonic devices

These produce bursts of ultra-sound which, while not at a high enough level to produce pain in the dog's ear, will hopefully startle him and divert his attention from the problem behaviour. Some are battery-operated instruments which are simply pointed at the dog.

TRAINING OLDER DOGS

You may be lucky when you 'inherit' an adult dog in finding that he already knows some of the common command words like 'Sit' and 'Come'. Dogs can retain a memory of human words for some considerable time, certainly six months, after they were last given. A recent paper in an American scientific journal described a Border Collie named Rico who had learnt a human vocabulary of 200 words and could remember the name of an object for a month after last hearing it. Even more impressive was her ability to interpret a small collection of words strung together in a phrase such as 'Fetch the sock for Granddad'. After hearing the command she would go off, find the garment and present it to the old gentleman. Here was a dog who could answer what is in fact a triple combination command without any sign of confusion.

Years ago I acquired a brace of sparky little Lancashire Heelers of whose history I knew virtually nothing. They were adults in need of training and apparently had none of the common command words in their memory banks. Then one day my wife happened to use the word 'rats' in their presence. The dogs exploded immediately into a frenzy of action, scuttling frantically around, yapping incessantly with their eyes gleaming, looking for nooks and crannies big enough for them to squeeze into in search of rodent prey. No matter to them that at the time we were in the lounge of our thoroughly pest-free home. We had found one word they knew only too well and saying it never failed for years after to elicit the same response. Clearly the Heelers, typically for their breed, had been working animals.

With your newly arrived pet, training or retraining the basic behaviours and ensuring that you have control of your dog, is all that is likely to be necessary. It's up to you whether you decide to go on and train him to walk on his hind legs or, as used once to be popular, 'die for the Queen'. (I must ask my American friends if dogs in the USA ever are or were ever trained to 'die for the President'.) There are several ways to teach your dog the basic commands. Some are very similar, but there are also harsh, even brutal methods used by a few professional trainers and they should never be considered.

LENGTH OF TRAINING

How long will it take to train your dog? It is impossible to say. It depends on a number of factors: how much time and determination you put into it and on the genetic make-up and breed of the dog. If the dog is an excitable type, it is sensible to spend time burning off some of his energy by taking him for a walk or playing with him vigorously before beginning a training session. Professional trainers reckon that it takes them on average around six weeks to train an adult dog thoroughly in the basic behaviours. In contrast, clients of mine who train wolves need six months just to gain their trust before training proper can commence: wild animals are far more dangerous and apprehensive than domesticated dogs.

The animal's innate, inherited characteristics can either enhance or handicap the training process. A fascinating example occurred in Africa when British Border

A SUCCESS STORY

Max was a 15-year-old German Shepherd/Border Collie cross belonging to Catherine, a lifelong friend of my sister. By the time he was 10 months old he had had two previous owners, one who didn't bother feeding him and the other who 'couldn't cope' with him. He ended up in a rescue centre and that is where Catherine found and adopted him. As soon as she arrived back at home with the dog, the effects of his maltreatment became only too apparent. Displaying all the signs of separation anxiety and desperate not to be left alone he would grab a leg or an arm of someone leaving the house and try to drag them back inside. He was generally 'wild', stealing and destroying things even when the family were present. He never urinated in the house, but he did defecate once, and once only. It could have been a coincidence, but it was on the occasion of a visit to the house by a lady from the rescue centre checking on his progress. I wonder if he was afraid she had come to take him back.

Catherine began taking Max to obedience classes shortly after acquiring him and continued to do so once a week for a few years, but Max was a different, clearly more disciplined and happy animal, even after the very first session. Meet him today, a senior citizen, he is one of the gentlest, brightest, most obedient and balanced dogs you are ever likely to encounter. A great success! The approach used in the obedience classes was essentially that described in this book.

Collies were imported into Ghana to be used in herding the local sheep. The experiment was a failure! The Border Collies, highly intelligent and obedient sheep dogs in Great Britain, and the shepherds' favourite co-workers, simply could not be trained to drive the Ghanaian sheep. The reason was that African sheep behave differently to other breeds and do not flock. Consequently all the Collies' ingrained, natural abilities and extensive training were to no avail.

GETTING PROFESSIONAL HELP

Under what circumstances should you consider consulting a professional dog behaviour consultant? If you are having problems training your dog and haven't the time to try to remedy the situation yourself, you may find it useful to attend obedience classes or consult a behavioural specialist. The latter can be expensive and, critically, they vary enormously in their expertise and experience. Make enquiries as to whether the consultant has worked much with your breed of dog. If the bulk of their practice has been with German Shepherds and Rottweilers, they may not be the best person to advise on your precious Pug or Shih-Tzu. And it is important that they are used to retraining mature, possibly quite old, dogs, as may well be the case with your new pet. A good way of finding out is to talk to your vet, ideally when your dog is being checked over to ascertain whether medical conditions could be contributing to the problem. The veterinarian will know of, or at least know where to look for, suitable canine behaviourists.

There are also boarding training facilities where dogs can be sent away for a few weeks to be instructed at 'canine boarding school'. Again, such courses tend to be

Obedience classes take place in most towns and are useful training aids as well as being entertaining for dogs and owners. They also give both plenty of good exercise.

rather expensive, and although the dog may learn to behave very well in the school, problems often arise when he returns home where any still-existing faults in the family environment or in the attitude and approach to training of the owner can quickly cause the progress made to collapse. Some boarding trainers have reported that as many as 75 per cent of owners are not motivated sufficiently to change their own ways in living and working with their 'reconditioned' dog. We must never forget that the relationship between an owner and a obedient dog is a two-way one. Man trains dog, but dog must also train man.

Dog Whispering

Recently Dog Whispering, the canine equivalent of Horse Whispering, has arrived on the training scene. It is a psychological, almost in some ways, spiritual approach to the man/dog relationship, utterly humane, and essentially based on an intimate comprehension of the dog's body language. One of its foremost proponents is the Norwegian Turid Rugaas, who studied wolves and dogs and found that these animals use 29 different calming signals of body posture, action or facial expression to avoid conflict. Dog Whispering training involves the dog and his owner developing a mutual understanding of each other's feelings and needs. It is about interpreting and responding to the dog's body language and also understanding how he thinks. The calming signals (see above) include yawning, tail wagging, blinking, sniffing the ground and turning away – behaviours often taken as acts of disobedience or at least disinterest by owners. Not so, claim dog whisperers. An example of dog whisperer training is how to deal with an aggressive dog. You must blink, turn away and stand still. The dog (hopefully, say I) will at once recognize your actions as 'calm down!' signals. Consultants practising this art can be located in pet magazine advertisements and on the Internet.

NOT TO BE USED UNDER ANY CIRCUMSTANCES

Never use collars that pinch or choke or are fitted with little blunt spikes to cause discomfort to the dog when the owner tugs on the lead. The bigger the tug, the more discomfort and pain for the dog. Neither should heavy chains be used as leads. Training, as ever, should be by positive reinforcement: by reward, not through inflicting suffering.

Nor should you use shock collars, which are sometimes activated by a remote control held by the owner to give the dog an electric shock. The intensity of the shock can be varied and some collars are fitted with buzzers or vibrators that precede the shock and give the dog the opportunity of desisting from the unwanted behaviour, thereby avoiding pain. This barbaric way to treat animals has thankfully all but disappeared and should not be condoned under any circumstances.

TIPS FOR SUCCESSFUL TRAINING

- Older dogs usually take longer to train or retrain than youngsters because of their ingrained habits. Be patient and bear this in mind if you acquire an older dog.
- Train the dog in various behaviours but only one at a time.
- Never try to train your dog if you are in a bad mood. It may upset him, especially if he is young. And never lose your temper with him.
- Rewards during training may be in the form of food titbits although some trainers prefer not to use food but praise, petting and play instead. That would be my choice, too. If food is used, it must be prepared in very small, pea-sized pieces and still be accompanied by praise and petting when given.
- It is vital that food rewards, when used in training, are given immediately the dog responds correctly to a command. Never give rewards when he performs some desirable behaviour of his own volition, only when he does so after a command. Food rewarding can be gradually reduced in frequency as training progresses.
- Accompany reward and punishment with verbal signals like 'Good dog!' and 'Bad dog!' Eventually these will be sufficient reward and punishment in themselves.
- Punishment must be used sparingly and of the correct type and must be given in a way and at a time that will associate the punishment with the misdeed. Punishing a dog for something he did some time earlier is counter-productive.
- Older dogs may be better re-trained at training classes.
- Training sessions should last no longer than 10 minutes for puppies and 20 minutes for adult dogs. The first sessions should only last five minutes and can be repeated several times daily for the first few days, before you move on to 10 minutes.
- Do not let your dog get bored by training for too long without a break.
- Do not let other family members interfere with a training session; it may be confusing for the dog. Decide on one person who is going to be responsible for training. The rest of the family can learn the commands later. They can engage in play, praise etc. as usual.
- Use a firm but gentle tone of voice to give commands and always use the dog's name to gain his attention before giving the command.
- Keep your voice pleasant and use the same, clear, single words for verbal commands.
- Begin training with the dog on a lead.
- When out walking, particularly with a young dog who is undergoing training, do not stop to talk to other people, do not allow lamp post sniffing, do not avoid other dogs, but just keep on walking, and do not go among traffic and crowds too soon.
- Always keep your dog on a lead near traffic and farm animals.
- The methods are the same whether you are training a young or an old dog.

Brothers and Sisters, I bid you beware
Of giving your heart to a dog to tear.

KIPLING, THE POWER OF THE DOG.

THE
BASIC
COMMANDS

5

Here is a guide to teaching your dog the basic commands, so that he can become a well-behaved and much-loved member of your family. They are not difficult to carry out but you will have to put aside some time every day and have plenty of patience. Indeed, training your dog can be an enjoyable experience for both of you.

As I have touched on, the basis of training is obedience, and indeed we often hear the phrase 'obedience training'. You can help dogs in difficulty and dogs in danger (such as an unruly dog who wants to chase cars) if you are able to guide them in such situations with commands such as 'Stay, 'Wait' and 'Sit'. Of course if a dog is to learn you must gain its attention and the first exercise is exactly that – a way to gain and keep your dog's attention.

Watch

1 Grab a treat and gain your dog's attention by holding it near to your face and speaking or calling his name until he looks at you (make sure he knows this is a treat you are showing him – if necessary bringing it close to his face for a few seconds then take it away).

2 Wait a few seconds with the treat held high, keeping his attention.
At this stage your dog may even sit for you, but don't worry if he doesn't.

3 Reward him with the treat if your dog remains focused on you and the treat, and pet him so he knows that he has done a good job.

Repeat 1 and 2, waiting for a longer period of time and if your dog remains focused for these longer periods, reward him again. If he looks away or becomes disinterested, hide the treat until he looks up at you (he will no doubt be wondering where the treat is). Then reward him again. This is a good exercise to begin a training session.

1

2

Sit

1 Hold a small morsel of food in front of the dog's nose.

2 Move it slowly and steadily up and over his head. The dog's nose will almost always follow the lure upwards while his rear end moves down to the floor and into the 'sit' position.

As his bottom makes contact with the floor, say 'Sit' and give the food.

NOTE: Do not hold the food too high or the dog may jump up for it instead of sitting. After not too many repeat performances you will find that merely sweeping your hand upwards without a food morsel will produce the 'Sit' response. From that point on, you should use the 'Sit' command before giving the dog something he wants, like a toy or a walk outside.

FOOD REWARDS

Never offer chocolate drops or pieces as 'rewards' for dogs, for whom it is toxic, due to the chemical theobromine which it contains. It can cause diarrhoea and vomiting and at high enough doses, is fatal. Toffee and candy should also never be given as treats.

THE BASIC COMMANDS

Down

1 Begin with the dog in the 'Sit' position, ideally on a smooth (but not too slippery) surface rather than a carpet or rug. Show the dog the treat.

2 Move the treat/ morsel of food downwards from in front of the tip of his nose to the floor immediately in front of his toes. Too far away and you may stimulate him to stand and walk towards the food.

3 When his front end eases down onto the floor, say 'Down' and give the food reward. Very soon, as with the 'Sit' command training, the hand movement alone, without a food morsel, will evoke the correct response.

1

2

3

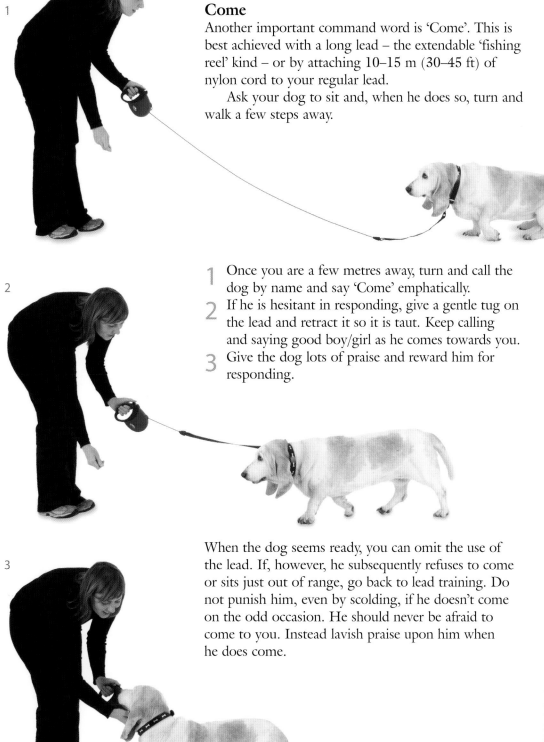

Come

Another important command word is 'Come'. This is best achieved with a long lead – the extendable 'fishing reel' kind – or by attaching 10–15 m (30–45 ft) of nylon cord to your regular lead.

Ask your dog to sit and, when he does so, turn and walk a few steps away.

1 Once you are a few metres away, turn and call the dog by name and say 'Come' emphatically.

2 If he is hesitant in responding, give a gentle tug on the lead and retract it so it is taut. Keep calling and saying good boy/girl as he comes towards you.

3 Give the dog lots of praise and reward him for responding.

When the dog seems ready, you can omit the use of the lead. If, however, he subsequently refuses to come or sits just out of range, go back to lead training. Do not punish him, even by scolding, if he doesn't come on the odd occasion. He should never be afraid to come to you. Instead lavish praise upon him when he does come.

Stay

Once your dog will sit on command you must introduce 'Stay'. Use the command along with a visual signal – extending one arm away from your body, palm of the hand upwards, towards the dog. This psychologically reduces the distance between you.

1 With your dog walking to heel on the lead, stop, make him sit and turn to face him.

2 Command 'Stay' and walk one step away from him, still with your hand held out.

If the dog moves to come to you, stop the exercise and go back close to him. If he stays, reward him with a treat and go on to 3.

3 Go two steps away from the dog. Keep your hand held out, saying 'Stay'.

4 Now try the 'Sit-Stay' command without the lead, gradually extending your distance from the dog. You can develop this command, by turning your back to your dog and also go further away until you are out of sight. When you return, praise your dog for his obedience and walk on.

TRAINING BLIND AND DEAF DOGS

Training a blind dog

If you have a blind or severely visually impaired dog, It is an act of good, caring ownership to teach him certain simple behaviours. This reduces his fearfulness and stress and creates confidence, helping him to stay out of trouble. He needs to know three basic commands: 'Slow down', 'Wait' and 'Sit'. It is not a difficult procedure, but at all times you must be patient and never give any sign of being exasperated or cross.

◆ 'SLOW DOWN' is necessary to avoid bumping into things. Put the lead on your dog and when he begins to walk pull back gently and steadily – do not jerk – and give the command 'Slow down' at the same time. When he slows, say 'Yes!' and reward him with praise and a food treat.

◆ 'WAIT' will help him to avoid dangerous situations, such as crossing the road or approaching an open manhole. Attach his lead and pull back gently but firmly, saying 'Wait' at the same time. When he stops, reward him as above. Don't begin training the 'Wait' behaviour until he has fully mastered 'Slow down'.

◆ 'SIT' will be used in a variety of situations, such as when you stop in the street to speak to a friend. Teach him by saying 'Sit' while holding a food treat near his nostrils. Slowly take the treat up over his head. When the dog sits, say 'Yes!' and reward him.

Training a deaf dog

This is not as difficult as you might imagine. Use signs – it is useful to obtain a booklet on American Sign Language – and facial expressions. Although your dog cannot hear you it is good to talk while signing; he will very soon learn to watch both your hands and face. Training sessions should last no more than around 15 minutes. To get his attention when you begin, stamp on the floor, wave your arm or flash a pen torch. Vocal praise cannot be used as a reward, but your dog will soon recognize clapping your hands, smiling and saying 'Good!' as signs of your pleasure at his behaviour. The key rewards for deaf dogs are food treats. Some deaf dogs know up to 50 signs by the time they are five or six years old.

Walking to heel

It is important that your dog learns to walk to heel at your side on a lead without pulling. A 2 m (6–7 ft) foot long lead is best for this with only about 1 m (3 ft) of it being used with the rest in reserve for paying-out if necessary. Until the dog gets the idea of all this, which usually doesn't take long, walking down the road can be a display of choreography that may incline passers-by to the view that you are rehearsing for a Come Dancing competition!

Put the lead on your dog, speaking reassuringly and calmly. Hold the lead firmly in one or both hands. With large and old dogs it is best to do this with a harness and training lead (see page 64). Do not permit lead chewing. Shorten the lead and bring the dog into the required position with his right shoulder beside your left leg.

Begin to walk in a straight line, saying 'Heel' firmly as you start. Continue talking pleasantly to your dog to reassure him that all is well even though he may at first wonder what is going on.

4

5

1 If he pulls forward or hangs back, stop. Do not let your dog drag you along.

2 If he does pull, turn around through 180 degrees and call your dog. If necessary gain his attention with a toy so that he comes back to you. The dog is now obliged to follow you; praise him when he does so.

3 As he comes back to you, bring his head level with your knee and turn him round to the right.

4 Keep him moving round, so that he is not tempted to sit. If necessary, give him verbal encouragement to keep him moving.

5 Continue to walk in the direction and at the pace you were originally going before your dog had other ideas.

The lead must never be taut. Make any turns carefully and restrict yourself to right turns – away from the dog. Turning to the left may trouble him at first as he may worry about becoming entangled with your legs. Introduce left turns only when he is accustomed to walking on the lead.

KEEPING CONTROL WHEN WALKING TO HEEL

You may find that your new pet is not well trained to walking on the lead, either straining forwards and pulling you along or hanging back reluctantly. If the dog is an old one, it may have had some unpleasant experience associated with a lead in his past life. Patience on the part of the owner is required, never punishment or the use of unpleasant devices like spiked collars.

Training the dog to walk at heel as described earlier is the ideal solution. Dogs that pull strenuously are frequently dominant types and it occurs more frequently in certain powerfully built breeds like Chows and Huskies. It is important to realize that when the dog pulls and the owner follows, it is the owner who is being trained and the act of quickening the pace briefly to catch up with the dog actually reinforces its behaviour. Correcting the fault can best be done by attaching the lead to a halter-collar, or even better, a harness with training leads attached to both ends. Gentle, not violent, tugs on the lead turn the dog's head (if using a head-collar) and small frequent tugs on both leads (when using a harness) help to keep the dog in check. When it pulls, the owner must give the tug and change the direction of walk. A pocketful of rewards in the form of food treats is essential, to be given together with praise as the dog relaxes, stops pulling and walks alongside.

A dog, usually a puppy, that is reluctant to move on the lead and hangs back, is treated slightly differently. Where the lead itself produces signs of fear in the animal, put it on it when feeding the dog in the house and let it trail it around. A lead around 6 feet (1.8 m) long is best. Don't use the retractable, 'fishing line' type of lead at this time. When you first go out for a walk avoid pulling hard on the lead if the dog is unwilling to move, as this will only frighten it further. Walk ahead of the animal to the full extent of the lead, crouch on your haunches or bend down, clap your hands once and praise the dog. The tone of your voice must be reassuring and happy, without any hint of irritation or impatience. If it doesn't move give the lead a quick tug or two. Should this fail, change the direction of walk by going behind the dog and repeating the procedure crouched in that position. When the dog does respond, give a food treat straight away. This system works reasonably quickly and a daily practice session will usually resolve the problem well within a week.

Some dogs will roll over on command, or walk on their hind legs. Find what your dog enjoys doing and let him have fun doing it.

Advanced training

Beyond obedience training, many owners may wish to go on to further, advanced teaching of certain behaviours. Common ones include rolling over, begging and standing on the hind legs using the methods of encouragement and reward described earlier. This can only increase the bonding, enjoyment and interest of both dog and owner.

Dogs, ye have had your day.

HOMER, ODYSSEY

OLD
DOGS

6

In older dogs, instances of unwelcome behaviour caused by their psychological or social circumstances are relatively infrequent – in one survey only six per cent of cases referred to animal behaviourists were dogs over nine years of age. Medical conditions lie at the root of many of their problems and owners should always seek veterinary advice before consulting an animal behaviourist if they are concerned about their pet's behavioural abnormalities.

Nevertheless, some elderly canine behaviours are expressions of a conservative, averse-to-change attitude which is similar to that commonly seen in old people. Aggression in the old dog may be as a result of physical conditions producing pain or irritability, but not infrequently the cause is possessiveness and a reluctance to give up a dominant position in the face of the new. The arrival of a baby, a toddler or a new pet can trigger this. A new, younger dog is a challenge to the old-timer who fears losing his dominance, and the owner who, understandably, takes the side of the old dog and perhaps scolds the young newcomer when it takes liberties is, in fact, making the situation worse. A change in the hierarchical position of the animals will happen. It is inevitable, and peace and amity will return once their positions in the hierarchy are resolved – by the animals themselves.

A new young pup in the household can help combat mental deterioration in an old dog.

ANXIETY IN OLD DOGS

Although they are experienced in life and set in their ways, old dogs often exhibit signs of anxiety that can involve problem behaviour. They can become more irritated by or fearful of changes in their environment, unfamiliar people or pets. And if you inherit some deceased relative's pet, any display of separation anxiety is, in essence, a form of grieving.

The anxiety lying behind many old dog behaviours may be a product of the animal's physical infirmity. A dog that simply cannot help producing an excessive quantity of urine may become anxious about soiling the house. It is not, as owners so often say to their vet, 'becoming dirty'. As the senses of sight and hearing fade with age, elderly pets may become anxious and stressed and the onset of cognitive dysfunction (see page 79) may increase the likelihood of anxiety attacks. They are often fearful of being separated from their owners whom they cannot see or hear clearly. Separation anxiety can lead to disturbed sleep periods with night-time howling, house soiling, destructiveness and, sometimes, compulsive behaviour patterns. Of course, restlessness at night may also be caused by medical conditions.

Noise phobias, likewise, sometimes seen when a new source of sound such as a CD player is installed in the home, can be due to a dislike of the new, the disturbing, but they may have their root in age-related changes in the animal's sense of hearing, although eventual complete deafness, if and when it occurs, will reverse the situation.

EFFECTS OF AGEING

Advancing age affects all parts of the body and each affected part may induce changes in the dog's behaviour, as outlined below. If you suspect that your dog may be exhibiting symptoms of one of the following or that changes in his behaviour may be due to physical ageing, you should consult your vet.

Digestive system

Dental disease, common in old dogs, particularly if regular inspection and teeth cleaning to prevent tartar and scale build-up have been neglected by the owner, can produce pain that then leads to irritability and even aggression. Older dogs sometimes suffer from bowel troubles, and constipation or more liquid stools may result in involuntary house soiling.

Respiratory system

Weakened, less efficient lungs reduce oxygen levels in the body, thereby decreasing energy and possibly producing a tendency to confusion during the night and senile changes in the brain.

Heart and blood

Some degree of heart disease exists in one-third of all dogs over 13 years of age. An inefficient heart restricts the ability to exercise and work. As with old humans, many elderly dogs are anaemic. Reduced oxygen levels associated with chronic anaemia may lead to senile changes in the brain, causing clinical signs such as apathy, increased daytime sleep and decreased responsiveness to stimuli.

Liver
Reduced liver function with age means inefficient destruction of circulating waste products in the blood. This can then induce brain pathology with associated behavioural changes of the kind described later when I deal with cognitive dysfunction (see page 79).

Urinary system
Kidney disease can cause excess urine production with resultant incontinence as well as retention of urea and other waste products that can affect the brain. Disease of other parts of the urinary system may affect an elderly dog's bladder control. An enlarged prostate gland can lead to constipation and/or urinary incontinence with consequent house soiling.

Hormonal system
An under-active pituitary gland may result in increased irritability or aggression, increased restlessness, over-eating, over-drinking, incontinence or house soiling. An under-active thyroid may decrease the dog's tolerance to cold. Tumours of the testis occur in around 60 per cent of older dogs with possible sexual aberrations including behavioural changes.

Bones, muscles and joints
Loss of bone density and muscle mass can decrease mobility and lead to house soiling. Arthritis and related diseases cause pain and irritability in old dogs.

The senses
Failing sight and hearing can cause anxiety, reduced responses to certain stimuli, fear, aggression, changed sleeping/waking cycles, increased vocalizing (barking), or hypersensitivity depending on the degree to which the sense has been lost.

The brain
The brains of both man and dog change, physically and in function, with the passing of the years. Old dogs may show signs of mental deterioration such as increased irritability, a slow response to commands, confusion, reduced

RELATIVE AGES OF MAN AND DOG

One year of a dog's life is often said to be equivalent to 7 of a human being's. In fact, it is more complicated than that, as this table shows:

		MAN (YEARS)		
		45–59 yrs (middle age)	60–74 yrs (elderly)	Over 75 yrs (geriatric)
DOG (SIZE)	Small (under 20 lb)	ca. 7 yrs	ca.11 yrs	ca. 15 yrs
	Medium (20–50 lb)	ca. 7 yrs	ca.10 yrs	ca.14 yrs
	Large (over 50 lb)	ca. 5 yrs	ca. 9 yrs	ca. 12 yrs

reaction to stimuli, disorientation, reduced interaction with and less interest in their owners, incontinence, forgetfulness (of once well-learned behaviours), lowered responses to sensory input or changes in their routine sleeping/waking cycle. If one or more of these exists without apparent physical cause, they can be described as being cognitively dysfunctional. If the changes advance and multiply to the point where a dog no longer leads a normal life, he is almost certainly suffering from senile dementia similar to that of human beings.

At post-mortem the brains of such an animal shows pathological changes more or less identical to those seen in cases of human Alzheimer's disease. Some of the drugs that are useful in giving relief to human Alzheimer sufferers have also been shown to have beneficial effects in combating and slowing the onset of cognitive dysfunction in dogs. Including fish oils and antioxidants, such as vitamins C and E, in the dog's diet is now thought to help in preventing and, perhaps, ameliorating cognitive dysfunction in old dogs (see page 81).

HANDLING BEHAVIOUR PROBLEMS

Firstly, pay regular attention to your pet's physical condition. Arrange for three- to six-monthly veterinary check-ups. Many of a dog's geriatric medical conditions can be treated by modern veterinary methods. The pain and inflammation of skeletal disease can be combated by new analgesics, corticosteroids and anti-inflammatory drugs similar to those used in afflicted humans. Urinary system conditions can be much alleviated, if not fully cured. A range of state-of-the-art clinical techniques, including ultrasound and electrocardiography, can investigate heart trouble, and in certain cases dogs are even being fitted with pacemakers. Surgery can deal with unwelcome tumours and tooth and gum problems, while operations to remove cataractous lenses from blind eyes are increasingly common.

Get to know the newly arrived old dog as soon as possible. Spend as much time with him as you can and check his bodily condition regularly.

Handle your dog frequently so that you become familiar with its body and can detect developing abnormalities early.

1 Make sure your dog is used to you inspecting his mouth, first simply with your finger. With care, lift back his lips and expose the teeth and gums.

2 Once your dog is accustomed to your finger being near his mouth, use a finger brush to sweep along the teeth.

Handle him frequently, watch him move and pay particular attention to the condition of his eyes, ears and mouth while grooming him. Make a point of doing regular weekly inspections, perhaps once a week while he is lying at your feet in the evening. The more you are familiar with the normal look, feel and behaviour of your dog, the quicker and more easily you will detect something going wrong.

Brush his teeth once or twice a week using an ordinary toothbrush or a special one that attaches to your finger, and canine toothpaste (available from your vet or pet shop). The technique is the same as for your own. Sweep the bristles along the length of the tooth away from the gum margin, first of the inside and then on the outside surfaces of the teeth. Use a soft toothbrush for young puppies and toy breeds, and a medium hard one for all other dogs.

Run your hands over his body to pick up signs of lumps, bumps or painful places. See that his toenails don't overgrow and, when necessary, have them promptly trimmed. Most important of all is to provide a suitable diet for the venerable creature.

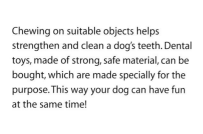

Chewing on suitable objects helps strengthen and clean a dog's teeth. Dental toys, made of strong, safe material, can be bought, which are made specially for the purpose. This way your dog can have fun at the same time!

Importance of grooming

Regular grooming is part of responsible dog ownership. It removes dead hair and cleans and stimulates the skin and hair follicles. Daily grooming is recommended when a dog moults (usually in Spring and Autumn, lasting 4 to 6 weeks). Certain breeds with different coat types, particularly those with silky coats (Afghan hounds, Maltese, Yorkshire Terrier, setters, spaniels and Pekingese) need particular attention.

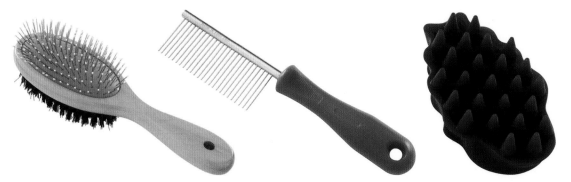

USE A BRUSH or a wide-toothed comb over the whole coat. Brush as required for the breed type, following the 'hair streams'.

USE A FINE-TOOTH COMB under the chin and tail and behind the ears. A wide tooth comb can be used over the entire coat for long-haired breeds or matted fur.

BRUSHING is easy with specially designed brushes, which make the hair cling to the brush which is useful during the moulting season.

THE OLD DOG'S DIET

A well-thought-out diet can lengthen a dog's life, slow the onset of mental degeneration and even improve behaviour in individuals exhibiting cognitive dysfunction. Proprietary brands of dog food, containing antioxidants, essential fatty acids and other beneficial chemicals, are now available for old dogs and can be bought in pet shops and from some veterinary clinics. If you prefer to make up your own dog food here are some pointers:

- As he grows old, the dog's kidneys and liver become increasingly less efficient in metabolizing food. The owner often first notices this when the dog begins to lose weight. Make sure you give your dog enough food if his appetite is good. Feed him to his satisfaction, not yours.
- Provide easily digested foods, such as fish and poultry – often.
- Give extra vitamins, particularly Vitamins E and C. Where a dog is beginning to show signs of mental deterioration give 25 milligrams of Vitamin E per kilogram of body weight per day and 10 milligrams per kilogram of Vitamin C.
- Keep drinking water available at all times.
- Use bran to combat any tendency to chronic constipation, and liquid paraffin (mineral oil) for one-off bouts of constipation. Be careful when giving liquid paraffin (mineral oil), particularly to frail old-timers: it is important that none goes down 'the wrong way' into the windpipe. Pour it slowly, teaspoon by

teaspoon, into the pouch formed by gently pulling out one side of the dog's lower lip, and letting him swallow frequently.

◆ Add fat (lard, chicken or turkey fat) to the dog's diet to provide extra calories for lean, elderly dogs: one teaspoon for small dogs; four for larger breeds.

◆ Fruit and vegetables in regular small quantities also supply valuable antioxidant chemicals. Fish oils contain essential omega-3 fatty acids that protect brain cells and have been found to be useful in treating senile dementia in human patients. They can also make a valuable contribution in the prevention and treatment of old age joint conditions.

Loss of appetite

If your dog is losing weight and has little appetite, it is best to seek veterinary advice as soon as possible. Like some old people, there are dogs that, while not suffering from any particular physical ailment, just lose interest in feeding. Reduced expenditure of energy in exercising plays a part in many cases of senior citizen inappetence. If this is the case, try tempting your dog with a variety of tasty morsels. The one I swear by for both cats and dogs is sardines in tomato sauce (not olive oil or brine).

Crumbling a yeast tablet onto his food before serving can also increase some dogs' appetites. In some cases, the vet may prescribe anabolic steroids for poor appetite and weight loss when there is no underlying physical cause.

Of course, appetite loss may be a sign of some form of underlying ailment. Conditions as varied as sore throats, tonsillitis, gastritis, kidney disease and liver malfunction can drastically reduce a dog's interest in food. I know one case of a spaniel, which, unknown to its owner, swallowed a tennis ball and, rather like obese folk who have inflatable balloons placed in their stomachs to cut down their desire for food, subsequently lost its appetite, and much weight as well!

HOME PREPARED DOG FOOD

The special proprietary foods for old dogs are fine, but if you would prefer, perhaps only occasionally, to cater personally for your pet, here follows a good, brain-preserving, recipe for canine veterans. The quantities given are per 10 kg weight of dog. You need the following ingredients:

$1/3$ cup rice

$1/2$ cup medium fat meat

$1/2$ cup wheat bran

1 tablespoon leftover cooked green vegetables and carrots

6 teaspoons raw liver

1 teaspoon steamed bone meal

1 teaspoon corn oil

$1/2$ teaspoon iodized salt

Two or three times a week, substitute fish or chicken for minced meat. Boil the rice in water. Mince the meat yourself (don't buy ready-minced meat for your dog – it can contain too much fat) and cook it in a little water. Mix into the rice and, when cool, add the other ingredients.

NOTE: Give Vitamins E and C at the dose rates mentioned on page 81 in capsule or tablet form each day. Also give one fish oil capsule or teaspoonful per day for small dogs, two for medium-sized dogs and three for big dogs.

MODIFYING UNWANTED BEHAVIOUR

After dealing with the physical side of the problematic geriatric dog we can now turn to other things that can be done to modify specific types of unwanted behaviour, particularly by you, the owner. You need to display a special understanding and patience with an old-timer, and it goes without saying that punishment is, again, out of the question at all times. Here are some useful guidelines for ways you can care more for your old dog:

1 Where the dog's faculties are declining, particularly those of sight and hearing, handle your dog gently, taking care not to startle him with sudden loud noises.

2 Make sure that your dog can see you before you switch on household appliances such as the vacuum cleaner.

3 Check behind your car before reversing outside your home in case the dog has got outside.

Completely blind dogs generally manage very well if their owner is thoughtful and patient. Indeed, a dog's excellent hearing (if deafness has not also set in) combined with his memory of the floor plan of your house may actually make blindness difficult to spot. Blind dogs can go for walks as usual but will probably stay close to you. Help by speaking to the dog frequently and not re-arranging the furniture more than necessary. If you have to leave a blind pet alone in the house, the sound of a radio will reduce his degree of isolation.

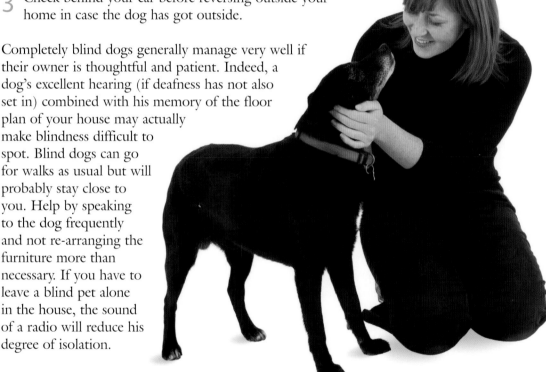

Avoid looming over your dog. Approach him from the front, stroking under the muzzle. This is especially important for deaf or blind dogs.

Separation anxiety

As we have seen, medical problems can induce anxiety in elderly animals, but separation anxiety may mean that the pet cannot be left alone for as long as previously. To allow him to relieve himself, ask a neighbour to pop in during the day. Other possibilities are installing a 'dog flap' in a door or putting down a 'litter box' plentifully lined with paper, which the dog can be encouraged to use. It usually doesn't take long for him to grasp the idea. A pheromone plug-in diffuser (see page 142), although somewhat more effective on young dogs, may also be helpful.

House soiling

If anxiety, a medical condition or cognitive changes lie behind a dog's soiling habit, the cause has to be identified and appropriate action taken. Medical problems can create on-going difficulties: for instance, an obese or arthritic animal may have difficulty negotiating stairs. Individuals producing excess amounts of urine (polyuria) due to chronic urinary ailments may just have to be given access to the outdoors more frequently. A period of re-training is called for. You will need to watch your dog carefully and immediately take him outside at the first sign of urination. A new routine with a timetable for 'being let out' should be set up, with rewards given to the pet. If the dog must spend fairly long periods of time indoors without access to the outside, a paper-lined litter box placed away from areas that were previously soiled may be used.

Disturbed nights and restlessness

Any medical problems that might interrupt the animal's sleep pattern have to be dealt with, although this can be difficult with some chronic conditions. Some old dogs, like many old people, are insomniacs. Giving the animal more exercise during the day, particularly in the evening, can be useful. To avoid reinforcing unwelcome visits by a restless animal during the night, he should be shut in his room, otherwise, the more he gets a response by waking you, the more he will do it. Sleeping tablets, such as diazepam (Valium), may be of value but would need to be prescribed by a vet.

Excessive vocalization and destructive behaviour

In some cases due to medical problems or cognitive dysfunction and in others as a consequence of separation anxiety, phobias or fear, these kinds of behaviour can be dealt with in old dogs as discussed for dogs in chapters 8 and 11.

Give your restless or insomniac pet plenty of exercise during the day, to burn off excess energy.

Aggression

It is vital to determine what kind of aggression your dog is exhibiting. Medical conditions that cause aggressiveness can be treated but symptoms in some cases, such as osteo-arthritis, cannot be totally eliminated. Sensitivity to touch with irritability and crotchetiness leading to displays of aggression can persist.

A young dog may challenge an older dog for their position of dominance in a household. This hierarchical jostling should be permitted, and dogs allowed to work it out in time, without interference from humans.

Fear-triggered aggression can be tackled by gradually de-sensitizing the animal to the causal stimulus and training the dog to respond promptly to your commands so that you are in control when the stimulus is present. We have discussed anxiety, another possible cause of aggressive episodes. In some cases a vet may advise giving anxiolytic (anti-anxiety) medication to such animals.

In old dogs social factors can lead to aggression. The arrival of a new dog, particularly a younger one, can lead to anxiety and apprehension in the existing pet. He becomes jealous of any attention the new arrival receives and fearful of losing his position in the family/pack pecking order. In these circumstances the pup and the old timer should be kept separated when there is no human supervision available. The pup should be given plenty of exercise so that tiredness wears out his 'bounciness' when he is with the older animal. Rough play should be discouraged, perhaps by distracting the pup with some toy or by means of a quick squirt from a water pistol. Gentle play, however, should be rewarded. A long lead and head halter on the pup can be helpful until he becomes trained and obedient to your voice commands. Don't forget that both animals are simultaneously going through a time of training and/or retraining.

CASE HISTORY: DEAFNESS AGGRESSION

Whisky was a 15-year-old West Highland Terrier who began snapping unexpectedly at members of the family for no obvious reason. Without warning he would lunge at a passing ankle or a hand stroking his back. Previously an amiable, perfectly behaved pet, his owners wondered whether he was becoming bad-tempered because of senility. If they had known of the condition, they would have suspected cognitive dysfunction.

Brought to the vet, Whisky was thoroughly examined and the possibility of deafness became significant. Yes, said the owners, he was perhaps somewhat less attentive these days. It was decided to give the dog a deafness test. He was very lightly anaesthetized to a level where a pair of normal ears would react by flicking in reaction to the stimulus of a sudden sharp sound. An alarm clock was placed near his head as he drowsed away and the button pressed to sound the alarm. No reaction: Whisky and his ears were oblivious to the noise. He drowsed on. Examination of the outer ears with an auriscope showed no evidence of disease there, so a diagnosis of deafness due to old age and changes in the middle and inner ears which were untreatable, was made.

The owners quickly came to see that the deaf terrier was snapping because he was constantly being surprised by unexpected touches and the sudden appearance of objects in front of his face without warning. From henceforth care would have to be taken not to surprise the dog and, more importantly, to approach him if possible from the front where he could see you coming. They resolved to develop a simple sign language with which to communicate with him. The family members devised and practised a small series of finger, hand and forearm signals that indicated 'Come', 'Stay', 'Good boy' and 'No' but also more elaborate messages like 'I am going to stroke you now' and 'Roll over so I can brush you'. Within one week of family and dog first employing the sign language, Whisky was a changed, patently happier character. He never snapped again and died eventually at the ripe old age of 21.

Whisky's case can be compared to that of an old Labrador I treated many years ago. She too had started snapping without warning for no good reason and her disobedience to voice commands was totally out of character. Auriscope examination at my surgery revealed unusual blockages in the depths of both outer ear canals. Polyps the size of large peas were completely obstructing the passage of sound waves. An operation under general anaesthetic to remove the polyps, a form of benign tumour, was completely successful. The Labrador bitch snapped no more.

Another form of aggressive behaviour is sometimes seen in households where two dogs have lived together amicably for many years. As the older dog develops medical and cognitive dysfunctional conditions, the younger animal may challenge him for hierarchical position, becoming 'pushier' when seeking favours from humans or becoming possessive of food or favourite bits of territory. Owners should not make matters worse by intervening in favour of one dog or the other. Rather, let them sort things out gradually for themselves. More supervision or separation of the dogs may be required as well as feeding and sleeping places for both animals in equally prestigious positions. Muzzles can be useful in some cases to avoid snapping injuries. Owners should provide intensive obedience training for both dogs as well as joint walks, games and other physical exercise.

Compulsive and stereotypical behaviours

In the old dog the majority of such cases are due to medical or cognitive dysfunctional abnormalities. If anxiety is the main factor, you should look for and correct the cause of the animal's 'worry' and provide alternative stimuli to distract, interest and calm him. Drugs prescribed by the vet may be required in some instances. See page 144 for advice on specific compulsive disorders of the dog.

Phobias and fears

We discussed how decline in sensory perception in old dogs can induce phobias, gradual deafness leading to noise phobias, for example. Keeping the dog away from annoying stimuli, masking them with background music (both cats and dogs do seem to prefer Classic FM!), and training the dog to rest and relax in a peaceful, stimulus-free zone are all effective measures that you can employ. Again, drugs may be indicated in certain cases under veterinary supervision.

COGNITIVE DYSFUNCTION (CANINE ALZHEIMER'S)

Like some old people, there are dogs that continue to be sprightly and alert into extreme old age, but most do not. Big dogs don't live as long as the smaller breeds. While few Great Danes, for example, go beyond 11 to 12 years of age and Labrador retrievers are seldom around to celebrate their fifteenth birthday, it is also true that small and medium-sized dogs reach 'old age' and can be termed 'geriatric' at 10 years old, although some 'geriatric' animals show no signs of mental deterioration for many years after that point. Some terriers bounce along until 20! The oldest dog on record was an Australian Cattle Dog that died in 1939 at just over 29 years of age. In 2002, a Collie in Somerset, England, fed on a vegan diet scoffed an appropriately vegan twenty-seventh birthday cake! (Interestingly, the domestic cat, which averages some 16 hours of sleep out of every 24, more than any other mammal, tends to enjoy a longer life than its canine colleagues. Incidentally, the longest-lived cat, as reliably recorded, was a tabby queen from Devon that achieved 34 years, although there is an unverified claim of a cat from Dumfriesshire, Scotland, dying in 1972 at the age of 43.)

Symptoms

These are many and can occur in a variety of combinations and to variable degrees. They include increased sleeping time, reduced active periods, lack of interest in the world around them, including their owners, reduced responsiveness to owners' commands and apparent increasing disobedience often manifested as seeming deafness (although true loss of hearing may be involved), confusion, difficulty in recognizing familiar humans, forgets his or her name, reduced interest in eating, loss of bowel and bladder control, increased difficulty in navigating their familiar environment and 'getting lost' in the house, aimless wandering, increased thirst, excessive panting, years of house-training undone and episodes of agitation or barking for no obvious reason.

Of course, some of these signs may not originate in the brain but have medical causes elsewhere in the body and you will need veterinary help to sort things out in your particular pet. We must never forget that a dog showing signs of cognitive dysfunction is not behaving that way on purpose, through peevishness or because it has lost his love for his family. The changes in his brain are physico-chemical; he can no more help acting as he does than dear old Aunt Agatha with her similar condition which has appeared with advancing years. The family must – and will – cope with both an increasingly eccentric dog and aunt. Neither is becoming mad or bad.

Causes

The condition is steadily progressive and leads eventually, but perhaps after some years, to complete incapability. Why do some dogs suffer from it and others not? Genetic factors probably have a major influence but diet and environmental factors may also play a part.

The effects of old age physical changes in the brain seem to stem from a reduction in the amount of a chemical called dopamine in the brain tissue. Dopamine is involved with the essential transmission of the nervous impulses that act as electrical messages to the body. Low dopamine means loss of messages that should stimulate activity and reaction by the dog to the environment.

Treatment

Recently a non-addictive drug, selegiline hydrochloride, that increases the levels of dopamine in the brain and is used in the treatment of human Parkinson's disease patients, has become available. It reverses the signs of brain ageing and strongly boosts cognition and awareness. Two out of three geriatric dogs treated with this drug under veterinary supervision have shown significant, even remarkable, improvement in their condition.

As is the case in old human beings, keeping the mind active and stimulating intellectual processes can play a vital role in warding off senile mental deterioration in a pet. With both dogs and men in later life, the motto must be: 'Use it or lose it'. You can do much to help your dog in achieving this: change his toy regularly, play new games with him, and vary the routes of your daily walks. All these things stimulate interest, attention and thinking in the canine brain. Buzzing brain cells really do wither and decay much more slowly than idle ones.

CASE HISTORY: COGNITIVE DYSFUNCTION

Josh was a much-loved German Shepherd living near my home in Surrey. Taken to obedience classes as a puppy, he grew up to be the perfect family pet, impeccably house-trained, charming with strangers and gently protective of young children in the household. Within the space of a few months, however, when he was 10 years old, Josh's behaviour began to change. His owners described him as 'day-dreaming', prone to inattention towards them, even when called. Previously a sound sleeper from about 11 pm till 7 am, he began rousing the family in the wee small hours by noisily pawing doors and other woodwork and barking intermittently for no apparent reason. He was uncharacteristically crotchety most of the time. Occasionally and totally out of character, he would cock his leg on the fridge or oven door in the kitchen. Finally he took to wandering off, seemingly with no predetermined destination. To the owners' consternation he was sometimes found lying resting in the middle of a busy road and, on one unforgettable occasion, strolled through the open doors of a church during the Sunday morning service, urinated in the main aisle and was preparing to curl up on the steps of the chancel when a church-warden, with the dog catching tongs that were standard equipment in mediaeval churches, and with considerable trepidation, hooked his mace of office in the dog's collar and ejected him.

Subsequent veterinary examination of Josh revealed no physical problems, merely some cloudiness of the lenses of his eyes. It was decided that he was showing signs of cognitive dysfunction and 30 milligrams of selegiline was prescribed for him to be given once a day. The dog showed little change in his aimless, forgetful, nocturnally noisy ways for about two weeks, but then things began to change distinctly for the better. The old Josh reappeared and episodes of incontinence ceased. He stopped wandering, was attentive and obedient just as in the old days and he reverted to sleeping quietly all night long. It was therefore decided to reduce the selegiline to a maintenance dose of 10 milligrams a day. Josh's improvement was maintained. In a very real sense his 'youth' had returned. He has lapsed only in the sense that he no longer attends church!

Dogs are not generally apt to revenge injuries inflicted upon them by their masters; but Mr Sikes's dog, having faults of temper in common with his owner, and labouring, perhaps, at this moment under a powerful sense of injury, made no more ado but at once fixed his teeth in one of the half-boots.

CHARLES DICKENS, OLIVER TWIST

AGGRESSIVE DOGS

7

Aggression is the undesirable behaviour for which owners most commonly seek professional help. It is also the most dangerous and disturbing and, although obviously a potential nightmare when involving a Dobermann, Rottweiler or Bull Terrier, any breed, even the fanciest and most petite, can be affected. In the USA alone some 5 million people are bitten by dogs each year, 15 to 20 of them fatally. The American insurance industry paid out 345.5 million dollars in dog bite claims in 2002. Children are the most frequent victims of aggressive dogs, and the commonest site of bites is the face. The two worst breeds for biting are reportedly the Rottweiler and Pit Bull types with 80 per cent of biting dogs being male.

The most aggressive animal on the planet is, of course, Man, and his frequently terrible displays of aggressive conduct come in a multitude of forms and have a broad spectrum of causes. Domestic dogs, likewise, can exhibit a variety of undesirable aggressive behaviours but like all other non-human animals, including killer whales, tigers and great white sharks, are not capable of the one type of aggression peculiar to *Homo sapiens*, that motivated by pure evil. There are at least 15 types of canine aggression and sometimes a dog can be afflicted by more than one type at the same time. These are explored in detail in the following pages.

DOMINANCE AGGRESSION

This type of aggression is most common in pedigree males, usually under four years of age. It is not very likely to occur if your 'inherited' dog is a senior citizen, particularly as he is now in a new pack and his old hierarchical position is no longer valid. One study found that the English Springer Spaniel is the breed most commonly referred to behaviour consultants for aggression towards owners in the United States.

Causes

We have considered the hierarchical nature of wolf society and the fact that the domestic dog brings some of its inherited lupine characteristics into its new pack, the owner's family. The dog is instinctively aware of its position in the social hierarchy whether it be *vis-à-vis* other dogs or human family members. Its position in the pecking order at any given time can be influenced by the nature of the challenger threatening its dominance and the type and degree of challenge that it perceives it is facing. Age, the state of its health, and its hormonal situation can play a part. If the dog feels that it is in danger of losing control of a situation or a physical resource to an individual, canine or human – it has hitherto considered a subordinate, it may attempt to reassert its status and a display of dominance aggression can ensue.

AGGRESSIVE BREEDS

BREEDS THAT TEND TO BE THE MOST AGGRESSIVE:
Small terrier breeds, German Shepherd, Rottweiler, Dobermann, Chow, Boxer, Afghan Hound, Husky, Samoyed, Schnauzer, Dachshund, Chihuahua.
BREEDS THAT TEND TO BE THE LEAST AGGRESSIVE:
Bulldog, Basset Hound, Retrievers.

These two dogs are squaring up for a fight, with both dogs equally matched in size and dominance.

Warning signs

There is a ritual to all this, not unlike the preludes to medieval battles where the opposing forces faced one another with trumpets blaring, banners streaming, knights posing bedecked in all their armoured finery upon their charges and the lines of yeomen shouting threats and cheering, all before at last clashing in combat. The dominant dog adopts postures and behaves in a way that boasts and threatens, a sort of canine *braggadocio* in the hope that the animal or person who appears to have taken liberties will back down, retreat or display some obvious form of deference. If they do not, the situation may escalate to a physical attack.

The signs that indicate a dog is in a dominant, trigger-happy mode are the maintenance of unblinking eye contact, lip retraction, holding the head and body as high as possible, the tail held above the horizontal, rigid tension of the body muscles, hackles raised and forward rotation of the ears. Additional signs if the opposition is another dog are: pushing over, slamming, mounting, standing over, placing the head or paws over the body of the other, and seizing the muzzle or neck of the other in its jaws. When in a dominant mode regarding humans the dog may attempt to control their movements, push them forcibly or block their path. Most often there is also some growling.

Observation of your pet's demeanour and body language is a constant necessity. If you are not aware of or ignore these premonitory signals, biting may occur and subsequently some owners may claim that it was 'unprovoked'. A dog should always be given a chance to make a signal. You should never rush to touch or otherwise interact with a pet and, when a warning signal is observed, it should not be ignored.

A subordinate dog, anxious to show his willingness to knuckle under and avoid a scrap, has a range of signs that he can display. They include: lowered head and tail, ears rotated backwards, crouched body position, lying on his side, avoidance of eye contact, retraction of lips horizontally, and urination. All in all, a big cringe worthy of a canine Uriah Heep.

Triggers

The dominance aggression behaviour will appear when triggered by some stimulus perceived as a challenge to the dog's status, particularly on the part of a family member whom the animal considers a subordinate, such as a child. Any dominant signal from a human, such as moving, handling, or approaching either themselves or something they regard as theirs, food or a toy maybe, can cause an aggressive response, especially if it occurs when they are resting, being groomed, hugged, stroked or simply stared at. They don't like being rudely interrupted.

Although dominance aggression is commonly thought to be challenge-related, it may be that in some, perhaps many, cases, anxiety or fears lie at the root of it.

MEDICAL CONDITIONS CAUSING AGGRESSION

Although some pathological processes that cause pain or illness and subsequent irritability and even aggression, particularly in old dogs, have been mentioned elsewhere in this book (arthritis, cognitive dysfunction, etc.), some other diseases can be factors in aggressive behaviour in any age of dog. They include the most notorious of all, the dreaded infection with rabies virus, brain tumours, ear and dental conditions, wounds, an underactive thyroid gland, various forms of neurological disorder including epilepsy, and the effects of badly tolerated medication or poisons. Treatment of these forms lies in the hands of the veterinary surgeon.

I am thinking particularly of the dog's worries about his position within the pack/family hierarchy or erratic, perhaps conflicting, signals from his owner or owners. One might imagine that the most likely exponent of dominance aggression in a pack would be the 'top dog'. This is not necessarily so, provided their position is settled and stable and other factors such as age or infirmity are not an issue. And, naturally, the 'under dogs' at the bottom of the social pile aren't prone to throwing their weight about. It is the animals in the middle orders, the ones still trying to sort out and uncertain of their relative niches, that are more likely to show this type of aggression. Insecurity can have a similar effect among groups of human beings under certain circumstances – teenage gangs and mobsters, for example.

Pain or discomfort produced by a medical condition or being handled in a certain manner may at times cause dogs to exhibit the signs of a dominant aggressive animal. The dog learns that a defensive, 'aggressive' response produces results by stopping the unpleasant experience. It has nothing to do with feelings of dominance.

Possessiveness on the part of the dog can also lead to behaviour that can be confused with or perhaps combined with dominance aggression. The dog threatens, growls and may even bite when approached by a person or another animal, perhaps even a cat, while he is in possession of food or an object which he considers to be his property. It can involve 'stolen' items and may be a defensive response in expectation of retribution if the dog has been physically punished on previous occasions for thieving. Possessive aggression occurs in both males and females and, although it can be found in dogs of any age, is commoner in adults.

One kind of dominance aggression that is particularly serious is the Rage Syndrome. Here severe outbursts of aggression occur with little or no warning. Rage Syndrome does seem to be linked to some form of genetic anomaly involving chemical processes in the brains of certain lines of dog, and is more commonly found in Springer Spaniels than other breeds.

Treatment

The key thing is to establish quite clearly in the dog's mind that the dominant pack member in the household is a human being. Following on from that it is essential to demonstrate that all persons in the family are higher in the pack hierarchy than the pet. This is done by obedience training given either by the 'pack leader' – you – or a professional dog trainer, and in due course by each and every member of the family. Obedience is synonymous with accepting the dominant role of the trainer. It is vital that the dog gets nothing he desires (food, attention, a walk) until he has responded correctly to an obedience command. While the training proceeds it may be necessary also to employ a muzzle or halter, and a long lead is always advisable

Training should include good rewards for obedience, acquiescence in handling and what can be termed subordination – evidence that the dog appreciates his subordinate status. The response to the 'stay' command should be developed to the point where it is strong. The dog should be instructed to 'stay' regularly and then, after a few moments, allowed to move, when going into, out of, or around the house. Physical punishment must *not* be applied. Apart from other considerations, it could be very dangerous.

Establishing basic commands such as 'sit' is key to gaining control of your dog.

USEFUL TIPS

1 Identify the situations or stimuli that trigger the aggressive behaviour. Keep the dog away from them or under firm control when they exist.

2 Do not reinforce attention-seeking and 'pushy' behaviour. Ignore it. Ignoring is a suitable punishment in many circumstances when dealing with this type of dog. There must be no angry confrontations between man and beast.

3 Keep the dog out of areas that he aggressively 'possesses', such as certain chairs, sleeping zones or your bed. Confine the dog to his own pen, bed or kennel.

When out of confinement and with you, use a long lead and halter to retain control at all times.

OTHER METHODS

Desensitization, the process of gradually reducing the dog's aggressive response to a trigger stimulus, can be done but there are risks and I think it best performed under the control of a behavioural expert on a one-to-one basis, and certainly not at an obedience class.

Other methods that may be of value in certain cases are veterinary ones. Castration of males can be advisable but where done, it must be accompanied by behaviour modification of the types outlined above to achieve success. The veterinarian, depending on a careful evaluation of each individual case and analysis of the underlying psychological factors, may recommend certain drugs. They include Prozac and similar anti-depressant medications, anxiety-combating, anti-psychotic preparations, and megestrol (incidentally my choice for treatment of the dominance aggression also sometimes seen in dolphins, whales and sea lions). This can be useful where aggression persists in some castrated males.

CASE HISTORY: DOMINANCE AGGRESSION

Jinx was a seven-year-old greyhound bitch adopted from the RSPCA by a client of mine, a fanatically dog-loving old lady, when I was in general practice. She had looked after the dog for almost six months when she came to see me with both her hands bandaged. She had left the greyhound at home. 'Jinx has gone funny on me,' she explained. 'Most upsetting. Snaps at me without cause. Taken over my bed so now I sleep on the couch downstairs. The RSPCA people say she was as gentle as a lamb with them. What do you think has gone wrong?'

I arranged to visit Jinx at home to see the situation in more detail. The dog turned out to be well-conditioned and healthy, but it was tricky for me to lay hands on her at first as she lay sprawled on the old lady's bed growling ominously. I asked the owner to tell me how she had treated the dog in general since she rehomed her. 'The best,' she replied. 'Food whenever she's peckish. Good food. Lots of stroking and cuddling whenever she asked for it. Not at all what I expected in a greyhound. I took her twice a day to the park for games. I always made sure she was happy. I let her win when we played tug-of-war with a leather strap. As you can see, I let her sleep on my bed. It's hers now. I suppose she thinks that, too. I tried to change the quilt again yesterday while she was on it and got another bite, just like last week. And, another time, she went for me when I moved her biscuit bowl.'

She raised one bandaged hand. 'The better I treat her, the more naughty she seems to have become. I suppose she's just defending things. I reckon that's natural.'

Jinx wasn't difficult to diagnose, but this was not simply a defence of territory. Unintentionally, indeed paradoxically, with the very best of intentions, the old lady had encouraged the dog by 'spoiling' her to act in a dominantly aggressive fashion. Giving her what she wanted whenever she wanted it, letting her 'win' every time, had reinforced a probably inherent dominance aggressive tendency. The dog was acting as pack leader, in pinnacle position in a mini-hierarchy of two, and regarded her owner as being a subordinate. The dog punished acts of insufficient servility and deference by snapping. She had, in effect, trained her owner.

The treatment was obvious. Not quite up to initiating obedience training herself, a professional trainer/behaviourist was called in. Within a matter of days, Jinx was brought under control and the hierarchical structure within the home was reversed. Jinx slept happily in a snugly lined kennel in the yard and waited patiently at all times for the few simple commands that the lady had been instructed in using, when they went out for walks on the Pennines.

POSSESSIVENESS AGGRESSION

Although possessiveness can be a feature of dominance aggression, it can be a completely separate phenomenon which is sometimes even exhibited by a dog who does not consider himself to be highest in the hierarchy. Some 'lowly' individuals have such a strong sense of ownership of food or an object, like a toy or slipper, that this overrides considerations of status. It occurs more commonly in adults than puppies and in both sexes. Typically the dog will growl and then lunge at someone approaching his marrow bone. It can be a significant problem in a household where there is little or no 'leadership' and dominance on the part of human beings and where there are young children or frail, elderly folk.

Treatment

Management of possessiveness requires you, the owner, to be more assertive in taking control of your pet – not by confrontation or physical punishment but by training of the type already described. Your leadership must be instilled into the dog, situations likely to encourage the behaviour must be avoided, and the animal trained to drop objects on command.

This is by no means as easy with an adult possessive dog as with a puppy. When feeding the dog, he should not simply be left to get on with it. You should accustom him to being stroked and talked to while feeding. Strangers can be asked to give the dog food at feeding time and a fuss made of adding favourite delicacies from time to time. Gradually the dog will come to realize that there is no threat to his food source and that no-one is going to steal it from him. Human beings will come to be associated with pleasurable feeding.

Lowly dogs should have their confidence built up, with the help of a behavioural specialist if necessary. Do not discount the possibility that they have been subject to an abusive previous owner. Certainly do not get angry with your dog if he displays possessiveness aggression.

'What's mine is mine! And don't you forget it!'. Make sure that your dog has toys and things that he can call his own, if you aren't happy with him harbouring your slippers...

PROTECTIVE AND TERRITORIAL AGGRESSION

Protection of the pack and the pack's territory is central to the behavioural characteristics of wolves and has been passed down over the ages to their canine descendants. The family dog knows the members of his pack and the boundaries of that pack's territory. Aggression towards non-pack members, human or animal, may occur when they approach or are within the perceived territory but may be totally absent when the dog is outside the territorial bounds.

This kind of aggression often has an element of fear within it and dogs with any tendency to timidity or anxiety in their make-up may even display what appears to be territorial or protective aggression when away from their territory, but it is actually better classed as a suspicious xenophobia. It is commoner in young dogs of both sexes. Some individuals seem more prone to territorial aggression than others, possibly because of genetic influences, and, as you might expect, the guard dog breeds are frequent offenders.

Many dogs regard any living thing outside the windows of the house as a potential threat to their territory.

Treatment

The question of Postman Pat is discussed elsewhere (see page 41). It is highly undesirable to allow a dog to patrol the family home boundaries behaving in an aggressive manner towards passers by. The dog that sits on the window-sill or dashes along inside the garden fence barking furiously and displaying many of the most threatening body and facial signals usually goes from bad to worse. From his point of view he is doing his job with great success; the 'enemy', scared off by the imprecations and abuse, does not usually enter the territory and indeed clears off.

If you have such a dog, you need to take full control of him and his environment. Guard dog breeds patrolling industrial premises are, I suppose, only doing their duty when exhibiting territorial aggression, but if they are kept as family pets, they should be encouraged to socialize, if possible from an early age, and should certainly not be left alone for long periods in a garden or yard. The window-sill barker and garden fence chaser should not be allowed to go into those places where they put on their displays unless you are present and taking control.

It is highly unlikely that your inherited dog will be one of these highly controversial 'designer' animals. They are, as yet, relatively few and far between, and in some countries like Great Britain, they fall under legislation concerning the keeping of dangerous wild animals. They certainly aren't the sorts of pets that dear old Aunt Gladys would be likely to bequeath to you.

The principal objection to these hybrids is that they tend to have an awful lot of wolf in them, including wolf behavioural characteristics. In them all the various types of canine aggression can often be writ large, particularly predatory aggression (see below), and there is a significant risk of serious damage to other animals and people, particularly children, who come into contact with them.

Control is often best exerted at first by means of a long lead and halter. A device such as a collar fitted with a citronella (lemon oil) spray activated by barking can prove very effective in controlling the noisiest individuals.

Physical punishment must *not* be used. As in most other forms of undesirable behaviour, training is the key solution. You must be able to gain obedience and calmness from your dog on command using the methods I have described in chapter 5, if necessary with the help of a head halter.

Gradual desensitization to the aggression-provoking trigger stimuli can be achieved by carefully introducing the animal to examples of them, at first mild ones, and then, building up slowly, to more challenging and powerful ones. Compliance and calmness should be fulsomely rewarded. A good method is play-acting and involves someone who is unfamiliar with the dog playing the part of a visitor with you inside the house and the dog on a halter and lead. The visitor knocks on the door, opens it and enters. You must have the dog under complete control. At the first sign of aggression, use an ultrasonic bleeper, air horn or rattle to give a 'stop' signal, and check the dog with the lead or halter. The visitor goes out and the scenario is repeated time and time again until the dog does not display aggression. Then it is time for you to give the 'Sit' command and a tasty food reward. Again all of this is repeated until it is possible to have the visitor, after entering and being accepted satisfactorily, give the 'Sit' command and proffer the reward.

PREDATORY AGGRESSION

Another form of aggression which originates from a dog's natural instincts is predation – the urge of the canid family to chase and kill prey animals. Although this is a normal part of a dog's psychology, trouble can arise when it involves 'hunting' other domestic animals and human beings. It can be displayed by dogs of any age and either sex.

Triggers

The behaviour is usually triggered by something in some way imitating the appearance, movement or sound of a prey animal, thereby arousing ancient responses deep in the dog's subconscious. It may be a quick moving object like a child in a pedal car, a cyclist, a motor vehicle or, of course, a running cat. They all tempt and remind the dog of 'dinner on the run'. The high-pitched cries of babies may also elicit a response. The screech of an animal often provokes a killing response. Wolves are known to kill fellow pack members that scream when caught in a hunter's trap, and the occasional tragic killing of an infant is often stimulated by its shrill cries when knocked down by a pushy, perhaps dominating, dog which up to that point had not been intending to bite.

Vehicle chasers are sometimes dogs whose instinct for territorial defence extends beyond the boundaries of their family home. If they are allowed to go out alone or are taken for walks in the neighbourhood where they regularly leave urine marks, they can come to believe that their territory also comprises the roads and streets around their home. They therefore treat invading strangers in the form of cars and bicycles moving around in the vicinity just as they treat postmen coming into the garden. It is not surprising that dogs of the sight hound breeds, such as Afghans and Greyhounds, have somewhat more of a tendency to chase vehicles than other dog breeds.

Signs

Once triggered, the dog goes into hunting mode, stalking, chasing and biting at the target, but he may call off the sortie at any point. In the worst cases a bite is administered, in the dog's imagination being hopefully a lethal one. Small children are particularly at risk from this sort of aggression. Some predatory dogs do actually kill other animals, such as cats and smaller dogs. The teasing behaviour of a cat or squirrel that regularly sits or patrols out of reach of the dog, perhaps in a neighbour's tree or on the roof of a garden shed, can build up frustration in a dog and lead to a killing attack on the provocative creature when the opportunity arises. The behaviour is especially difficult to eradicate if a dog is inherited that was used by previous owners to hunt and kill prey in some manner.

Treatment

Some fairly disgusting ways of tackling this have been practised in the past, including attaching the dead prey to the dog's collar and letting it remain there until it rotted away. (I am, to be clear, talking about small prey, not the grisly corpse of the old lady next door's late, lamented ginger tom dangling from your terrier's collar for a week or two!)

It is more effective to prevent the aggression by identifying the stimuli that trigger the behaviour and not exposing the dog to those stimuli, except under controlled conditions during training.

1 First try the muzzle over the nose to get your dog used to the feeling. Give him a break and try again.

2 Once he is used to the feel of the muzzle, place it over the nose, taking care to mind your fingers.

3 Fasten the muzzle behind the head, taking care not to trap fur in the clasp.

4 The muzzle should be a snug fit, but not pressing against the skin and with space inside the basket.

Obedience training with tight control by the owner is essential, using the appropriate equipment. Walks should be taken with the dog on the lead and halter, at least until training is complete and fully ingrained. Some dogs can never be fully trusted and will never be permitted to be off the lead during walks. Obviously, for this and a host of other reasons, the dog must never be allowed to go out unaccompanied and some animals may need a muzzle fitted whenever they are taken out by their owner.

Desensitization training

This involves the dog being exposed to the potential prey for short periods at least three or four times a week, preferably daily, with full control maintained by the owner by halter and lead and with voice commands. Correct, unaggressive, obedient behaviour must be rewarded by favourite food snacks, praise and petting and distracting little games undertaken while the potential prey stimulus is still present. Again, you must assert your leadership and this must be recognized by the dog who will come to realize that if his pack leader shows no interest in chasing cats or motorbikes, neither should he. Even so, it is very difficult to break the habit in some long-term hard cases.

REMOTE CONTROL DEVICES

These are recommended by some trainers, especially the ones attached to a dog's collar. These may allow you, the owner, some distance away, to deliver a shock or a puff of citronella oil vapour. I repeat that I consider electric shock techniques cruel, although the citronella oil gadget is perfectly acceptable. The vapour's smell is by no means offensive to humans though dogs don't like it. It merely acts as a harmless deterrent and should be used in conjunction with your voice command. It is clearly most effective when the dog is at least partially obedient to such commands. As soon as you see your dog preparing a display of aggression, you must press the remote control button and shout the command 'Stay' or 'Sit', then praise obedience.

CHASING CARS

I am unimpressed by some of the weird, wonderful and positively lunatic ways in which some owners have tried to stop their dogs chasing cars. These include squirting ammonia or lemon juice at the dog from a moving vehicle, shooting rock salt at it from a shotgun poked out of the window of a moving car, and spreading drawing pins over the roadway and then letting the dog chase cars.

MIXED SIGNAL AGGRESSION

This type of aggression, sometimes known as conflict related aggression, is most often seen in highly strung and easily excited dogs. There appear to be competing impulses operating simultaneously in the animal's mind resulting in the giving of contradictory signals. The dog may suddenly switch from a friendly approach to a display of aggression – often fearful, defensive aggression. An amiable, sociable pet in an excited state is suddenly frightened by some unexpected stimulus, such as a quick movement or gesture, and reacts aggressively. A friendly, tail-wagging approach to a person or another animal is mixed with abrupt, timid withdrawal, or a state of high excitement is mixed with elements of aggressive behaviour.

It reminds me of what parents often say to their over-excited children roistering exuberantly: 'Calm down now or it'll end in tears!' It often seems as if the friendly, happy dog has some sort of invisible limit or boundary surrounding him. Sudden intrusion by certain stimuli within that boundary generates fear or defensiveness which manifests itself in rapid alteration in his behaviour. 'So far and no further, please, otherwise I'll feel threatened!' These invisible limits are not geographically defined, although they may seem so. They are more a kind of mental territory with fragile boundaries that may collapse, especially when in states of high excitement.

CASE HISTORY: MIXED SIGNAL AGGRESSION

Jasper, a bouncy, bright-eyed five-year-old Wire-Haired Terrier was a fully paid-up member of a loving and caring family pack. He was friendly and welcoming both to visitors to the family home and to other people and animals encountered out on walks. He was always keen to socialize and play games indoors and out with both people and dogs. The trouble was that frequently, when the socializing or game reached a certain point and Jasper was highly excited, he would switch to being fearful in the twinkling of an eye and for no apparent reason. He backed off, cowered sometimes, and often snapped at the nearest living creature. The snap was more of a defensive warning than an attempt to inflict real injury. Battle was rarely if ever joined. Jasper usually calmed down quickly once he appreciated that the 'threat' was not a real one, but the fun and recreation was always over for that day.

The terrier was taken to an obedience class where the instructor quickly eradicated his unwanted behaviour by instructing the owners in the simple training measures outlined below.

1 It is important that the dog is not punished for becoming aggressive.

2 Before introducing the dog to situations (in Jasper's case, meetings with other dogs or strangers) that might trigger the behaviour, he must be trained to walk in a calm and collected manner to heel, and to lie down on command.

3 When this training is in place and solid, the dog can be reintroduced gradually to likely stimuli. If he gets excited, the training commands should be used to calm him down.

4 Rewards for compliance are, naturally, essential. An excited dog should be approached gently with a hand stretched out and a fist rather than fingers, before proffering a reward in the form of a food treat or petting.

5 All family members must know how to do all this and put it into practice permanently, not for just a few days.

PAIN OR AILMENT-INDUCED AGGRESSION

Aggression caused by underlying pain or illness is easy to understand. Think of what would regularly befall you should you accidentally step on grandma's chilblains. A dog will react to being touched or handled where a tender or aching spot is involved. Sometimes a condition requiring veterinary attention is first discovered when an animal that is normally more than happy to be picked up or stroked, yelps and snaps. This is even truer of cats that commonly develop painful acute infections under the skin after being bitten by one of their fellows. The fur hides the generally undramatic but agonizing swelling. The owner will arrive at the veterinary surgery complaining principally of an unusual irascible reaction without the slightest suspicion of what is really no more than a soft and flattish 'boil' being the cause. The first dose of an antibiotic usually dispels the animal's bad temper within hours.

Causes

Of course, old dogs are more commonly afflicted with this type of aggression than youngsters. Arthritic conditions and toothache are among the more frequent causes. Sometimes underlying illness produces aggressive behaviour not so much from points of physical discomfort, but rather by way of a general increase in the individual's general irritability. Chronic liver or kidney disease, hormonal disbalances and disorders of the central nervous system can all produce feelings of simply being unwell and, thereby, irritability. It is possible that these conditions can actually give the dog a headache, but we have no way of proving this.

Treatment

The way to handle such cases is obvious: treat any specific physical ailment and particular care on the part of the owners in touching and handling their dog. Dogs who from puppyhood have been accustomed to regular handling, grooming, tooth inspection and cleaning will usually be much more amenable to handling in later life when illness or infirmity arises.

Regular grooming of your dog will accustom him to being handled, inspected and so on. Your vet will also be very grateful: visits may be a little easier.

MATERNAL AGGRESSION

Another easily understandable form of canine aggression, and one commonly seen in many other animal species (the most ferocious displays of it that I have witnessed occurred in felines – tigers, cheetahs and, most outraged of all, domestic cats) is maternal aggression, a behaviour initiated by the instinctive desire of a mother to protect her young. It can be directed both at people and other animals that come close to her puppies, and it can also affect bitches showing the signs of false or phantom pregnancy when they typically will make a 'whelping nest' and take a slipper or old sock to be their 'pup' and jealously guard it against all-comers. Approaches that are considered too close to the puppies, whether real or imaginary, are met by growls, barks and even snapping. Bitches that have been well trained since their youth and which possess the social graces within the family are less likely to exhibit such behaviour. In most cases it fades away as the puppies grow older or the false pregnancy, a hormonal condition, abates.

Treatment

Tackling maternal aggression is not difficult. Handling of puppies, particularly during the first days of life, should be kept to a minimum. Gentle, cautious handling by the dog's favourite family member is normally very effective but some very aggressive bitches may have to be muzzled. Young children especially must be restrained from approaching or touching the puppies of affected bitches. If you can begin training to reinforce obedience and enjoyment of handling, grooming and petting well before the pups are born this is an often-effective prevention of the behaviour.

Of course, if you don't intend the bitch to have puppies, arrange for her to be spayed (the ovario-hysterectomy operation) before, but not during, her first heat (oestrus) period. Spaying also will eliminate the false pregnancy phenomenon, which in the worst cases can occur twice a year. (False pregnancies can also be prevented or terminated by contraceptive pills or injections as advised by your vet.)

AGGRESSION TOWARDS OTHER DOGS

Dogs fight for a variety of reasons, some of them particularly applicable to a new canine arrival in the home. It may be because of jealousy stemming from owner favouritism, territoriality, their 'ownership' of items of property such as toys and sometimes human beings, the presence in the vicinity of a bitch on heat, a critical lack of socialization with other animals during the first three to four months of life, or from having a dominant relationship towards their owners.

Some were bullies even while they were still young puppies in the litter; others have had experience of being attacked by other aggressive dogs or tend quickly to become highly excited when under stress. It goes without saying that one of the most despicable forms of cruelty inflicted upon dogs by man is the organised dog fight. Surprisingly, and very sadly, a survey in Chicago has found that one in six school students say they have attended such an event.

Sometimes two dogs living in the same household and treated even-handedly by their owners will fight. Most commonly the behaviour is first exhibited between

This visible display of aggression may result in both parties thinking better of entering a scrap. When in the vicinity of other dogs, aggressive dogs should be kept on a lead at all times.

one and three years of age in both males and un-spayed females. This is difficult to understand. It may be evidence of a struggle to assert some form of primacy in competing for the attentions of family members and where it occurs involving two bitches, an unstable social hierarchy complicated by the cycles of normal hormonal activity is probably at the root of it. Other possible factors contributing to its occurrence are a new dog arriving in the family pack, the death or infirmity of a once dominant dog, a younger dog deciding it is time to challenge the position of an older dominant individual, a dog returning to the home after being boarded or hospitalized, a human family member leaving home or a new member arriving. Tackling outbreaks of in-house warfare is usually far from easy.

Treatment
The rehabilitation of a dog with a tendency to fight can be very difficult. The first step must be to identify, if necessary with professional help, the kind of stimulus that provokes the behaviour. Whatever the cause, basic training by the owner to develop and reinforce reliable obedience and immediate response to voice commands is vital. In some cases, leads, halters and muzzles may be essential pieces of equipment.

Depending on the identified cause of the behaviour one or more of the following may be applicable:

1 Discouraging urine marking when the dog is taken out in the neighbourhood to avoid him extending his territorial area (and consequently the urge to defend it).

2 Avoiding dramatic and emotional displays or physical punishment by the owner when fighting occurs.

3 Distracting the dog by petting, praising and playing with him, preferably on the lead, when a stimulus appears.

4 Encouraging and reinforcing socialization with other dogs throughout his life, but particularly in the early weeks of puppyhood – not possible with the 'inherited' animal.

5 Avoiding potential flash points and providing lots of exercise to burn off energy and, incidentally, raise the serotonin levels in the body, are also important.

If two dogs in the same home tend to fight, the owner should try to identify the structure of the family pack hierarchy. All human family members must be in a 'dominant' position, exhibit leadership, expect obedience to commands and control access to desired things like food by insisting that a command is first obeyed.

A common error is to be over-supportive to the animal perceived as being in a subordinate position in the pecking order. The correct approach is to spend time encouraging the dominant individual to graciously defer and stop any tendency to challenge. Some dominant dogs seem not to understand or react inappropriately to submission signals from their subordinates and have to be taught the correct behaviour of acceptance and disengagement at such times. Control and leadership through training, usually with the aid of lead and halter (and muzzle if necessary) is, as ever, the key to success.

Two family dogs are less likely to start scrapping if they are both taken for walks on leads. A good method is for two family members to walk the dogs with them on leads and halters. Peaceful coexistence is achieved by at first arranging for the

Distracting your dog with a toy or game can help prevent encounters with other dogs turning violent.

I remember the case of a pair of male Boxers who had lived in utmost peace for several years with a young bachelor. When the man became engaged and his fiancée, a passionate dog lover, moved into his house, she lavished attention on the two Boxers, taking them for frequent walks and play sessions, grooming them assiduously and constantly buying them treats and tasty titbits.

The young lady's fondness of the dogs was quickly and completely reciprocated. I believe they both fell in love with her and, like rival human suitors, vied, one with the other, to be her favourite. Bouts of fighting started to occur on a regular basis. A behaviour consultant called in to solve the problem tried various approaches in modifying the dogs', and the humans', behaviour, but to no avail. Finally an American colleague of mine suggested raising the levels of a chemical called serotonin in the dogs' brains. Serotonin is involved in numerous neuro-chemical processes within brain cells and is a major player in mood and emotional functions. More serotonin, less aggression was the idea.

So the dogs were given daily doses of an amino acid, tryptophan, which is part of the manufacturing process of the brain's serotonin, together with a low-protein diet. I would much prefer not to use drugs in correcting behavioural problems, but on this occasion the medication produced excellent results. Fighting bouts were no more, and peace returned to man and dog in the household.

two people to walk together with the dogs on the outside. Then, as the walks continue over several days, one dog walks between the people, the other on the outside. Soon a point is reached where both dogs are allowed to walk shoulder to shoulder with the owners on the outside.

In some cases, and only on veterinary advice, castration of males that fight with other males and spaying of bitches that fight with other bitches may be the solution. Drugs such as serotonin-elevators or certain hormones are also of value.

DEFENSIVE (FEAR-RELATED) AGGRESSION

This type of aggression can vary in intensity from one individual to another. Its root causes are also varied and can include factors in the dog's genetic make-up, the memory of painful, unpleasant or frightening events, inadequate socialization during the first three to four months of life and, very importantly, unintentional reinforcement of the behaviour by the owner, past or present.

Fearful behaviour is much commoner in wolves than in dogs, which suggests that the process of artificial selection during domestication, with man considering fearfulness in an animal to be highly undesirable, has tended to 'breed out' excessive timidity. Bitches are slightly more prone to fear-related aggression than dogs.

As might be expected, neurotic and psychotic animals (psychologists have difficulty in clearly distinguishing between these two words, especially in dogs) that show other evidence of psychological abnormality, such as anxiety, hyperactivity and excitability or destructiveness, are also frequently affected by it. Medical factors that can induce psychosis in some cases and so lead on to fear-related incidents are traumatic injuries to the head, severe beatings, prolonged cortico-steroid medication and diseases, particularly when they occur in the puppy, that include distemper, chronic pancreatitis and heavy parasitism.

It is often said by owners that their pet hates going to the vet. I must say that over many years of veterinary practice I was rarely presented with a terrified, let alone a fearful, aggressive dog. It is among the exotic animals that vetophobia can be met in my experience. Primates, in particular chimpanzees and some gorillas, can put on a highly dramatic display when I come on the scene carrying my dart gun or blowpipe, even if the last time they saw me was years ago. Chimps – and elephants – never forget the vet.

Warning signs

The signs of a dog in defensive-aggressive mode are a mixture of body postures and facial expressions signalling both fear and the intention to attack. The ears are turned back, the tail is carried down and the crouching body is pivoted away from the causative stimulus. The body hair, particularly along the back, stands on end, the pupils are fully dilated, and the breathing rate increases. There may be growling, barking, snarling and, ultimately, biting. Some very scared dogs urinate or defecate.

Treatment

If a dog you acquire has been prone to this type of behaviour since he was a puppy, curing him will be far harder than in an adult that became defensively aggressive much later in life. It is always worse in a nervous dog that is frequently faced by fear-generating stimuli, particularly if he has little chance of running away. Such an animal may well bite and, if biting in the past has had the effect or apparent effect of driving off the stimulus, whether man or animal induced, the inclination to use his teeth may be reinforced.

In tackling this kind of aggression, the earlier you start the better. Firstly, identify the fear-provoking stimuli and, if possible, try to avoid them. Do not punish the dog; it can easily make matters worse. Do not unintentionally reinforce the behaviour by fussing over the pet and giving him treats when he exhibits the behaviour. As in most other forms of bad behaviour, owner control is of paramount importance. With, at first, the help of a lead and halter, obedience training or retraining can be reinforced and the dog gradually desensitized towards the causal stimuli by gradual, gentle, fully supervised exposure to them. The lead and halter prevent the dog from running off and from actually attacking.

Patience in all this is essential. Proceed cautiously; do not rush the training and reward good, i.e. calm, unscared, unaggressive, displays of obedience promptly. If you are responsible for bringing up a young dog, try to ensure that he socializes at an early age, meeting lots of different people and animals under pleasant, enjoyable conditions before he is six months old. Giving food treats during such encounters is an excellent way of the dog growing up to think nice things about strangers. Playing is an important part of these encounters with other dogs, and owners can be taken by surprise the first time they see their puppy play with another dog because of the vigour with which they engage with each other. This is all part of their growing up and developing healthy responses to other animals which can prevent problems such as aggression of different sorts fom developing.

For a few defensive-aggressive individuals, drug therapy involving anti-anxiety or tranquillizing medication under the supervision of a veterinarian may be necessary, but if at all possible should be avoided, certainly for long-term dosage.

CASE HISTORY: DEFENSIVE AGGRESSION

A curious and unique case was that of Charlie, a Cocker Spaniel owned by an acquaintance of mine. This dog utterly detested and was plainly fearful of television pictures showing darkly bearded men in close-up. No-one knew whether Charlie had perhaps been ill-treated by such a person at some time in his life, but whenever there was a shot of a face bearing an exuberant growth of fuzz on TV he would exhibit most of the classic signs of defensive aggression, including biting. The biting was, perhaps understandably, directed at the fascia of the television set. On one memorable occasion he closed down the family's evening viewing by biting and shattering the 'on-off' button while a learned and magnificently bearded Muslim scholar was talking about the American threats to invade Iraq. 'Seems like Charlie's a bit pro-Bush!' said his owner when next I saw him.

By good fortune Charlie was eventually weaned off his 'beardophobia' when a new neighbour with a carrot-coloured goatee came to live in the house next door. A keen dog lover, he introduced himself over the garden fence to Charlie, little by little, never teasing or provoking him and only when the dog was accompanied by his owner. At first Charlie flew into a rage when the goatee appeared above the fence, but gradually, as the days passed and the neighbour threw him biscuit treats, the spaniel changed his attitude to the point where he wagged his tail happily whenever he spotted the man. Through repeated, brief, unthreatening encounters he had become desensitized to the neighbour's beard and, it later transpired, to beards in general. Six weeks after taking up residence, the bearded neighbour began walking Charlie to the park.

PLAY-RELATED AGGRESSION

If the newly acquired dog is an adult, he is not likely to trouble you with episodes of play aggression – even less so if he's old. Play leading to aggression is a young dog's thing and really can be considered part of their normal behaviour, just as in children who often play 'too rough' as their parents will complain. The problems arise when a puppy's play proceeds from mock assaults of bumping, mouthing, gently biting, growling and challenging, to the infliction of significant damage in the form of harder bites, as well as uncontrolled jumping up and tugging hard on clothing. It is a problem for the whole family. Usually in the early stages there is none of the fixed staring, tense body postures and prolonged, lower-pitch growling seen in the more serious adult forms of aggressive behaviour, but nevertheless biting of any kind can be a serious matter for children and old people with tissue-paper thin skin.

Causes

Predisposing or contributing causes in naturally boisterous pups include the playing of aggressive, competitive games such as tug o' war with people, lack of obedience training, owner control and leadership, lack of exercise and play opportunities, playing with a puppy when he solicits a play session, thereby inadvertently reinforcing his behaviour, inappropriate behaviour such as chasing, scolding, striking out at or pulling away from the pup when he displays the behaviour, and, possibly, genetic factors. Apart from the latter, all of these must be avoided.

Plenty of exercise is key to maintaining a well-behaved dog. As with children, boisterous play among dogs can lead to squabbling but this is inevitable at times. Do not be tempted to keep your dog locked up indoors.

Treating play aggression

Things NOT to do when dealing with play aggression are:

1 Avoiding playing with the dog altogether.
2 Physical punishment, including running after the dog in an attempt to hit it.
3 Scolding – it will not be understood.
4 Rewarding or encouraging aggressive play as, for example, putting on gloves and then permitting the dog to bite happily away at your hand or trying to persuade him to stop the aggression by proffering a food bribe.
5 Engaging in play fighting with a puppy.
6 Leaving a very young child alone with a dog.

Things to DO when treating play aggression are as follows:

1 Gain or strengthen control of the dog through obedience training, perhaps going to obedience classes. All family members should be involved in some way.
2 Punish immediately by the use of a loud, sharp sound, such as from an air horn or police whistle. However, if the punishment causes fear, discontinue it.
3 When out with the dog play 'distance' games, such as throwing a ball or sticks, rather than ones that involve him taking part of your person or clothing in his mouth, even playfully.
4 Encourage play with other dogs – don't avoid contact.
5 Be strict and assertive with the dog in upholding your leadership and insisting on obedience at all times.

REDIRECTED AGGRESSION

This is, I suppose you could say, a display of unfair retribution, the directing of aggressive behaviour at someone or something that is not the stimulus. It is seen in cats, too, and is very much a case of 'Oi! Why clip my ear when he is the one that did it?' The classic case concerns the owner intervening in a dog fight or where the dog is acting aggressively towards some person and getting bitten. Another example is the dog furiously barking at a stranger on the other side of his fence and then lungeing at the owner who comes out and grabs his collar to restrain him. It is commoner in old rather than young dogs and can occur in pets of both sexes.

I think that in most cases, while in the heat of battle, the offending dog is too focused and preoccupied to distinguish between the flesh of his owner and his opponent. Usually such incidents are 'one offs', but with very aggressive dogs that frequently go to war, it can be difficult to eradicate unless the owner withdraws completely from the scene. In the United States 77 per cent of dogs that bite humans belong to the victim's family or friends, and 61 per cent of bites happen at home or in a familiar place.

Treatment

As ever, control of the dog is the essence of managing this type of behaviour together with taking prudent precautions. Potential problematic situations must be identified and avoided and, clearly, you should not get physically involved in any of the dog's aggressive engagements. It's just plain silly to put your hands into the middle of the melée. Keeping the dog on a lead when walking through 'enemy territory' or if 'the enemy' can actually be seen in the distance, is highly recommended.

Training to ensure obedience – full obedience – with the owner, not the stimulus, being the focus of the dog's attention, is essential and can then, with the dog on a halter and lead, (ideally a long retractable one that allows you to pull him back from a distance), progress to desensitizing sessions during controlled exposures to the stimulus. A muzzle may also be required. It is not difficult to divert a dog's attention from the stimulus when necessary by the use of a sharp signal from a horn or whistle. Reinforcing your dominance in the family pack by acting as pack leader (see page 29) is invaluable in these cases. Even when fighting a dog may be aware enough to obey the wise rule: 'Don't bite the boss!'. I am not in favour of using drugs to treat redirected aggression because of the risk of side effects from the medication, which so far have not, to my mind, been studied sufficiently in the treatment of domestic animals.

NOTE: One final cautionary note. All dog bites should receive professional medical attention. An awful lot of nasty bacteria make their permanent home in the canine mouth.

LEARNED AGGRESSION

This kind of canine aggression is entirely the owner's fault, either intentionally or inadvertently. Some dogs are taught to be aggressive, to chase cats or other animals, to act in a belligerent way when guarding premises or, not uncommonly nowadays, to participate in dog fights. I am sure we can assume that the dog you gave shelter to when dear old Aunt Agatha died isn't a Pit Bull Terrier that she employed to deter trouble-makers visiting the crack cocaine den she operated for all those years behind the lace curtains of Daffodil Cottage. Unintentional teaching of aggressiveness happens when owners reinforce an undesirable behaviour by reward of some kind, for example by petting the dog if he growls when frightened by some form of stimulus. Furthermore, the opposite type of behaviour on the part of the owner, punishing the dog in some way for displaying signs of aggression towards a stimulus, may have a similar result, causing him to link punishment and stimulus in his mind so that he becomes even more aggressive when the same situation arises in the future.

Treatment

The cure for such behaviour lies, of course, in changing the behaviour of the owner and, through obedience training, to gradually desensitise the dog to the stimulus and encourage and insist on correct conduct.

Gaining control through training will necessitate the use of a lead and, in some cases, a muzzle. Most importantly, the owner should not under any circumstances, try to calm or distract the dog with food treats, nor must any form of punishment be administered.

AGGRESSION TOWARDS FAMILY MEMBERS

I have covered the possible causes of aggression towards human members of the family. Aspects of defensive reaction, possessiveness, dominance and hierarchical status, experience of physical punishment or fear are some of the factors that are generally involved. Sometimes the aggression is only directed at family members other than the perceived 'leader of the pack'. The important thing is for owners to recognize the problem, understand the dog's point of view and modify the behaviour of all involved, both human and animal.

Treatment

Management of this behavioural fault requires correction of the identified causes existing in the household in the ways outlined earlier when dealing with specific forms of aggression. Then a two-phase regime is called for.

Firstly, all members of the family must adopt the 'cold shoulder' attitude regarding the dog. He should be given no attention apart from attending to his absolutely basic requirements – food, water, and toilet. No petting, no sweet words, no play time, not even talking to him or using his name nor making eye contact. Usually within three or four days the dog has become concerned about all this frigidity and comes asking, not pushily demanding – approaches in that manner must still be ignored – for petting and other overt displays of affection. At this stage the dog is commanded, pleasantly enough, to 'Sit'. When he does so, a little petting and praise is permitted, but it must be brief. Gradually more training of obedient behaviour within the house, such as following you, not leading, from room to room is introduced combined, of course, with avoiding the stimuli that caused the problem.

The second phase is what American behaviour consultants have termed the 'jolly routine'. It is applied as soon as it appears that the dog is on the point of becoming aggressive. At that instant, you must be ready to give a sharp signal, such as a hand clap, immediately followed by something jolly, the bounce of a ball, smiles or fulsome praise. This should be repeated until the dog instantly drops signs of impending aggression and reacts happily in anticipation, perhaps moving towards the person, tail wagging, before the hand clap can be given. This technique, if followed carefully by all family members, works very well indeed. The 'jolly routine' should not be used with animals that are predisposed to bouts of play aggression as it could trigger an attack.

AGGRESSION TOWARDS OUTSIDERS

The underlying cause of this type of aggression, which is aimed at people outside the family pack, is insecurity. The dog is uncertain of his relationship with the family, the family home and perhaps things within the home. A minority of cases may be the result of mistreatment or excessive teasing by strangers or, possibly unbeknown to others in the house, former family members, particularly children. The dog's bad attitude can be further enhanced if family members show signs of fear or aggression towards outsiders, if the social structure of the family pack is not clearly defined or unstable, if the dog's aggressive disposition has ever been encouraged by the owners in some way, if outsiders seldom visit the house or if the dog has for some reason been shut away from the family when they have visitors. Some cases of canine xenophobia are actually displays of over-protectiveness towards the family or its property, especially if, living with a single person, the dog senses their insecurity. A typical example of this rather praiseworthy behaviour is a rather timid old lady who has been recently widowed. Her pet dog notes the alterations, some quite subtle, in her behaviour since her husband's death – the changed daily routine, the no-longer happy atmosphere in the house, the downbeat, often morose conversation without the once familiar laughter when visitors call. Other cases are really only forms of territoriality inducing aggression.

Treatment

The approach to managing such cases is, after identifying and planning to avoid any trigger stimuli wherever possible, using the 'jolly routine' described on page 115 without the first 'cold shoulder' phase mentioned.

I suppose the little West Highland Terrier that we had when I was a boy was suffering from aggression towards outsiders, but one day when he was out walking with my father and I, we stopped to talk to the local vicar and the terrier promptly cocked his leg and relieved himself against the parson's trouser leg. Was that terrier territoriality in action? Was it anti-clerical aggression? Or was it a mild form of denominational aggression? After all Westies come from the Highlands of Scotland where Wee Free Presbyterians are rather sniffy about Episcopalians such as Anglican vicars.

The 'jolly routine' is an important part of treating aggression to outsiders and should take the form of praise, and cuddles.

IDIOPATHIC AGGRESSION

Many canine behaviour consultants recognize one further type of aggression in dogs. It is not common and its cause is unknown. Its scientific name, idiopathic aggression, is reserved for those cases where thorough veterinary and behavioural examinations have been unable to identify any causative stimulus. Brain tumours and the aptly named 'furious' form of rabies can produce identical behaviour.

One form of it can affect young adult dogs that suddenly change in character from being amenable to very belligerent frequently at around two years of age, a sort of Jekyll and Hyde scenario. The incidents of aggression, episodes of often the most violent rage, appear without warning and in the absence of any apparent trigger factor. It is interesting and rather alarming that electro-encephalographic examinations of such dogs have revealed brain waves very similar to those of wild beasts. Dogs suffering from this mysterious condition are very dangerous, in some ways the canine equivalent of human psychopaths, and treatment is impossible.

I have only seen the condition once, in a middle-aged Rhodesian Ridgeback belonging to a friend in France. He had lived happily in the family along with another Ridgeback from puppyhood and was perfectly well-behaved at all times, being particularly fond of my friend's year-old daughter. Without warning, something extremely disturbing occurred. One evening the dog, lying peaceably in beside the fire and surrounded by the family, suddenly changed into a totally different animal. It stood up and went at once into a menacing attack mode, body tense, eyes glaring intensely at my friend's wife, hackles raised, ears swung forwards, lips drawn back, and growling continuously. Just as it was clearly on the point of charging, my friend, who has years of experience in studying and modifying the behaviour of killer whales, intervened. (Surprisingly he wasn't bitten – but then in his professional life as Curator of Marine Mammals at a marine park he has to avoid killer whale teeth on a daily basis.) With no previous history of strange behaviour and a detailed medical examination revealing nothing amiss, the dog had to be euthanased. This is, sadly, always indicated in such cases.

PSYCHOTIC DOGS

There are a very few psychotic dogs whose behaviour defies explanation. With people they may display all the signs of a big welcome with lots of tail wagging and looking pleased, but their sole aim is to lure the unwary close enough to be able to take a large chunk out of them. There is no defence against such dogs as they give no warning hints. Fortunately, however, they are quite rare. Absolutely uncontrolled aggression in a dog is really too dangerous to deal with in most circumstances, and although absent from Great Britain, in many countries rabies must always be considered as a possible cause. Sadly, such animals are probably best euthanased.

DESTRUCTIVE DOGS

DOGS

Destructive behaviour in young puppies is part of natural development. They learn about things around them and strengthen their milk teeth by chewing objects. Similarly, mouthing things, especially the mother's breast, is one of the most important ways of connecting with the world around it for a human baby in the early weeks of life. However, if older dogs chew the leg off the grand piano or indulge in other acts of wanton destructiveness, their owner must identify and understand the reasons for this behaviour and then take measures to correct it.

Some breeds tend more easily to destructiveness than others if they are not given plenty of exercise every day. These include the following: Retrievers, Setters, Border Collies, Bearded Collies, Pointers, the bigger sight hounds, Dalmatians, Huskies, Weimaraners, Foxhounds and Coonhounds.

Causes

There are numerous possible causes. In some dogs it can involve 'mouth-type' stimuli such as being given chewable toys or chewable items of the owner's clothing, such as an old slipper, for them to use while the owner is absent, or the playing of tug o' war games. Physical punishment given too long after the damage was done, typically when the owner returns home, or using isolation of the dog as a punishment can induce even more of the same behaviour. Too much fuss and attention given to the pet when the owner is at home, sheer boredom, and frustration with retaining barriers, such as doors and windows, can all be factors. And as with other forms of unwelcome canine behaviour, poor or inconsistent leadership on the part of the owner and lack of socialization opportunities during the critical first three months of life are frequently responsible.

Regularly providing chews can help alleviate destructiveness.

REDIRECTED AGGRESSION

Destructive behaviour can also be a sort of redirected aggression towards the chewed-on object as, for example, in the case of the Bichon Frisé that was teased and challenged by a grey squirrel that came each day and ran up and down the kitchen window ledge. The little dog, emitting a sort of muttering squeal all the while, would spring up onto the counter top and snap away in his frustration and impotence at items of crockery and cutlery lying there. One day he cut his tongue on a knife and was brought to my surgery for treatment.

POSSIBLE CAUSES OF DESTRUCTIVE BEHAVIOUR

Here is a checklist of possible causes to be considered if your dog is behaving destructively:

- If a pup, is it just normal, boisterous, inquisitive play?
- Is the dog left alone for long?
- Does he get plenty of regular exercise?
- Do you play tugging games with him?
- Does he have plenty of regular socializing time with the family and other animals?
- Does he have toys that interest him?
- Could there be any reason for him to be anxious?
- Is anything or anybody stressing or teasing him?
- Has he been physically punished in the past for chewing things?
- Does he receive adequate quantities of food on a regular basis?
- Has he enough space?
- Do barriers such as doors, fences, and windows frustrate him?
- Have there been any loud noises? Industrial machinery, builders, thunder, fireworks?
- Is there a need for more obedience training within the family?
- Are you showing consistent leadership and control when you are with your dog?

NOW: Once you have an idea of possible causes and/or stimuli, eliminate them if possible and follow the correcting steps outlined on page 122.

SEPARATION ANXIETY

Separation anxiety may affect a dog if he is left alone for long periods, and the destructive behaviour will be frequently accompanied by incessant whining or howling (normally noticed by neighbours!) and a tendency for the animal to follow his owner around persistently when they return to the house.

REHOMED DOGS

You may know little or nothing about your newly acquired dog's past. He may 'have form' in one or more unwanted behaviours as well as destructiveness. He could even be a serial furniture gnawer. Anxiety is something that an inherited dog, young or old, is susceptible to in the first weeks with a new owner. The loss of the old home and family pack and the strangeness of the new regime can combine to affect the canine mind, and I think it is commonest in old dogs that have lived for many years with a previous owner.

IDLENESS AND HUNGER

Destructive behaviour may also affect the energetic, working breeds and a dog which lacks space, exercise, or sufficient time for play and socialization with family members. To paraphrase the old saying: 'The devil always finds work for idle dogs to do.' Clearly it is asking for trouble to keep one of the high-energy or big breeds as a pet in a bachelor apartment in an inner city high-rise block. Out of loneliness, boredom or frustration, the dog may well start chewing and destroying whatever is to hand. Sometimes the stimulus of a loud noise, such as fireworks or thunder, may trigger a bout of furniture wrecking. And then there is hunger, where perhaps the amount of food is reduced or feeding time is delayed. If peckishness is involved, the destructive urge is not normally directed towards the velvet curtains or Elizabethan prie-dieu but rather at something smelling of food, such as the larder door.

TREATMENT

Tackling destructiveness necessitates first identifying likely causative factors in the dog's daily life and environment. Some may be easily altered, but others less so. The following are some additional possible approaches.

1 The dog is confined in a place (or perhaps a crate or kennel) where it cannot do damage or be influenced by triggering stimuli (i.e. the squirrel on the window ledge) while the owner is away.

2 Maximum space and opportunities for exercise and play are provided. If you are out at work all day maybe a neighbour could pop in at lunchtime to take the dog for a walk.

3 Non-physical punishment of destructive behaviour should be given immediately it occurs when you are present. The instant the dog begins to chew at the inappropriate item, scold him gently but firmly or give a sound signal from something such as a horn or whistle. Cayenne pepper or bitter sprays, obtainable from your vet or pet shop, can be applied to household objects to deter chewing.

4 It is effective to give the dog non-household objects as chewable play toys, reinforcing his use of them by giving praise, petting or a titbit reward. Try out a selection of toys at first to find out which ones he prefers.

Exercise and games help relieve boredom, which can be at the root of destructive behaviour.

Chewable dog toys are made to withstand strong jaws. Some can be thrown (1), some are designed to be chewed (2). Others have pockets in which to place treats (3). or grooves to enable simultaneous teeth cleaning (4).

5   Chewable toys should be changed frequently – novelty maintains interest. They should buy toys designed specifically for that purpose, which are made of non-toxic material, able to withstand the surprising force of a Staffordshire Bull terrier if that is what you own.

DIGGING

Earlier I mentioned the jackal's habit of burying food (see page 41). All the canid family are keen diggers. The various species of fox dig to cache food for later retrieval (for the arctic fox cold storage beneath the snow seems essential for survival during the winter) and wolves are adept at excavating dens.

    The technique of excavating a hole is common to all the canids, including the domestic dog. The earth is removed by scratching alternately with the fore paws and the food or other item to be hidden is then pushed into the hole with the snout and is covered over by pushing earth over, again using the snout. Sometimes a domestic dog will go through the same sequence of digging motions where no earth is present, for example attempting to 'bury' a bone in an armchair or carpet. Some wild species, such as foxes and fennecs, have been seen doing the same on concrete floors in zoos. German Shepherds and sledge-dog breeds, such as Huskies, regularly dig holes for shelter and to escape very cold or very hot weather. Dogs bred to hunt prey underground, such as terriers and Dachshunds, had to do some digging when out working. Wolves are good at tunnelling under wire fencing, and many domestic dogs will dig to escape from gardens or other premises.

Causes

Undesirable digging, a form of destructiveness, in the domestic dog has a variety of causes that need to be identified if the behaviour is to be satisfactorily modified. It may be quite obviously a firm intention 'to get to the other side' where something interesting or provocative lies on the other side of a fence, say. I have known cases where dogs, with their highly tuned sense of hearing, could hear the movements of rats, mice or moles under the ground surface and wanted to investigate.

A large percentage of 'digger dogs' are, however, reacting to the same sort of causal stimuli that we discussed above in the section on destructiveness. Frustration, inadequate exercise or socialization, underlying anxiety of some kind, being thrown out of the house when visitors come calling, typically if the dog has other 'guest-welcoming' bad habits such as jumping up in effusive greeting or thrusting its nose into groins, or just plain boredom – any of these may be responsible.

There are also digging dogs that seem to have got the idea from watching family members tending the garden. No sooner has Dad finished turning over the soil around his radishes and gone indoors for a refreshing beer than the family dog continues the work, efficiently uprooting all of the plants. In his eyes, he is copying and helping a family pack member. Understandable, very thoughtful, but utterly unappreciated! With such assistant gardeners, it is wise not to allow them to be present whenever humans are digging holes.

Other possible causes include a desire for social interaction which is more common in larger, herding-type dogs kept in too small an area, sexual urge where the dog is trying to escape to find a mate, the instinct to create a den for itself where suitable shelter is not provided, boredom through lack of stimulation, anxiety, particularly separation anxiety when the animal is parted from its owner,

ENCOURAGING DIGGING

One last word about some canine diggers that are highly to be encouraged. There is a kind of dog that is employed by man to unearth one of the most sublime foods known to gastronomes, the white winter truffle, *Tuber magnatum pico*, a sort of underground mushroom growing close to the roots of certain types of tree. The home of the truffle is the area round Alba in Piedmont, Italy. There, in late autumn, truffle hunters go out with their highly valued, truffle-sniffing dogs to search for the elusive fungus, one of which no bigger than a golf ball can fetch a staggeringly high price on the London market.

The dog's exquisite sense of smell is the key to locating the buried treasure. Once it has pinpointed the spot, it will begin scratching at the soil with its forepaws. Up until fairly recently there was a University of Truffle Hounds for training dogs in this invaluable work (I speak as a white truffle fanatic) at the town of Roddi near Alba. Pigs, which are also blessed with a fine sense of smell, are also sometimes used for hunting the black summer truffle in parts of France. Only one man, (and no it wasn't Cyrano de Bergerac), has ever possessed a nose capable of picking up the faint aroma of truffle emanating from the earth.

frustration, when insufficiently stimulated and denied enough socialization time with humans or other dogs, obsessive-compulsive behaviour, and simply feeling unwell. Some dogs actually dig a hole in which to die. Breeds such as terriers dig as part of their hunting nature and, by means of their acute sense of smell and good hearing, go rooting for beetles, moles or, in the USA, groundhogs. Digging can become a form of attention seeking. If the owner shouts at the dog or regularly inspects its pen when looking for evidence of more excavation, the animal learns that digging gets the owner's attention. The solution to digging depends on the owner identifying the cause and taking appropriate action which may mean enlarging the space available to the dog, giving it more attention in the form of walks and play or perhaps exterminating the resident population of moles.

Treatment

Managing unwanted digging should firstly be directed at eliminating any obvious causes like those suggested above. A dog intent on digging out to go a-wandering, often a male in search of the local bitches, could be castrated. A nervous individual might take kindly to being provided with a comfortable kennel or a small hut of his own. Other persistent diggers may be let outside into a hard-floored dog run instead of being permitted to use the whole garden. If there is an area of the garden where you don't mind canine excavations, the dog can be encouraged to work there by burying toys and the like, or you could install a sand pit for the same purpose. In some cases, certainly not all, providing playthings like rubber rings, beach balls or a thick-knotted piece of rope dangling from a tree or fence can serve as effective distractions.

Otherwise you will have to train your pet not to dig up the prize petunias by interrupting him, preferably in such a way that you remain unseen and thus not connected to the interruption. Two possible ways of doing this are turning on a lawn sprinkler or activating a remote-control citronella-spraying collar.

Favourite digging spots can be covered with wire netting or filled with big stones. At first, while retraining a digging dog, you will need to supervise as much as possible his garden outings. As ever, obedience training with control by command, together with lots of exercise, socializing and game playing, are an essential part of the cure. Digging that damages furniture and carpet indoors should be tackled as advised for general destructiveness behaviour (see chapter 7).

In my view the most effective way of countering destructive behaviour is undoubtedly exercise – plenty of it and often. When a tired and happy dog returns home, it is far less likely to go on a furniture-chomping spree.

My husband says, if he doesn't stop cocking his leg on the grandfather clock, we'll have to have him put down. That clock was given to me by my grandmother.
A TROUBLED CLIENT TALKING ABOUT HER MANCHESTER TERRIER.

TOILET TROUBLES

The commonest complaint by owners about undesirable behaviour in their pet dogs concerns house soiling, urinating and/or defecating in the wrong place. (Cats are accused of it even more frequently.) However, what might cause this? We explore possible explanations in this chapter, together with advice on how to treat the problem.

In almost all cases, we assume that the dog we inherit is, or was at some time, house-trained, but with, say, a young animal that has spent much of its life up to now in a dogs' home, this may not be the case and full house-training will have to be implemented. There are four main types of inappropriate urination sometimes exhibited by dogs, and these are outlined below.

URINE MARKING

The impetus to leave a urine mark, a sort of olfactory staking-out of territory is common to all the canid family. The domestic dog cocks one leg and squirts a quantity of urine sideways against some object, more or less at nose height, to make it easy for the next sniffing dog that comes along to pick it up. All canid males and the females of a few species cock their leg. The urine smell conveys complex chemical messages concerning the identity of an individual and sexual status and, because it changes as time passes, tells the sniffer how long ago the urinating animal was there. For wolf packs the urine marking of the borders of their territory at regular points, and the subsequent refreshing of the 'keep off!' messages with more urine squirts when out on patrol is highly important.

The domestic dog urine marks to indicate his proprietorial rights, for hormonal reasons and also sometimes if stressed. An anxious or frustrated animal may mark if, for example, he is shut out of a room where he knows his owner is, or if he sees through the window a strange dog or a human visitor close to the premises. Some bitches will urine mark only when in season.

Treatment

Dealing with this behaviour involves avoiding or eliminating identified stimuli. You can administer non-physical punishment at once if you catch your dog in the act. A sharp noise or loud scolding word will often suffice. A remotely controlled alarm or citronella spray collar with you staying out of sight of the dog can also be very effective.

A remotely-controlled electronic device fitted to a dog's collar which emits a puff of citronella or sound can be a useful deterrent.

Rubbing your dog's nose in the urine patch is absolutely wrong as is punishing him some time after the deed was committed.

Obedience training, again, is central to correcting this habit and therefore, if the dog is checked successfully just before peeing commences, rewarding him with praise and petting him immediately will reinforce the good behaviour.

Naturally all urine marks should be cleaned and de-odorized. The dog's bed or food bowl can be placed at a marking site and, perhaps, he can be kept out of rooms where he is wont to go a-marking. If all else fails, castration of males will usually solve the problem, and females that consistently do it when in season can be spayed (but only when out of season).

PHYSICAL PROBLEMS

When a dog begins urinating in the home a thorough veterinary check-up is essential in case there is some form of disease present that is increasing the quantity of urine produced or the frequency with which the dog feels the need to pass water, or which is affecting his bladder control. I am not going to deal with the diagnosis and treatment of the various disease processes that can be involved in this, but they include the following: chronic kidney disease, diabetes (2 types), pyometra (a disease of the uterus), liver disease, over-active adrenal glands, urinary tract infections, tumours or stones in the bladder, prostate enlargement, abdominal tumours, damage or disease of certain types in the brain or spinal cord.

Treatment

Geriatric dogs may lose control of their bladders and, because of arthritis or weakness, have difficulty making it to the correct urinating place in time. Earlier we discussed cognitive dysfunction in old dogs. Separation anxiety generally afflicts these old timers more than younger dogs, so thoughtful steps must be taken to understand and adjust to their changing needs. They should not be left long on their own. Arrange for more frequent toilet trips and help the dog in negotiating stairs and getting outside. Avoid sudden changes in feeding times and daily routine within the family.

OVER-EXCITED URINATION

It is reliably reported by the cleaners that there are lots of wet seats in the auditorium when Mick and the boys walk off stage at the end of a Rolling Stones concert. Over-excitement leads to involuntary loss of bladder control, and so it seems with certain dogs that become highly aroused when rushing to greet their owner or some other friend. This is more likely to occur after a period of separation, isolation or general inactivity and can be reinforced by your reactions when the meeting occurs. Too much effusive whooping and fuss-making can simply make it more likely to occur again next time. Some dogs may have a genetic predisposition to over-excitability, and there are also those with weak control of their bladder valve.

Treatment

Correcting the behaviour means toning down your behaviour when you are greeting your dog, keeping your voice low and calm, and avoiding eye contact. You should also tackle any possible causative factors: give your dog regular exercise and socialization periods together and, if possible, do not leave him alone for too long. Obedience treatment is important, too. Distract the dog when he is about to launch into his excited display by giving obedience commands ('Stay' or 'Sit', etc.) or throw his ball. Take care if, on returning home after a period away, you bring presents such as treats for your dog. If you offer these at the meeting point when the dog urinates, they can be seen as rewards for the behaviour, which is thus reinforced. In those few cases where a weak sphincter valve in the bladder is the cause, a vet may prescribe drug therapy.

SUBMISSIVE URINATION

Avoid fussing over the excitable dog that urinates when he sees you.

This type of unwelcome urine voiding is commoner in young dogs and bitches, probably because the latter carry less of the 'macho' dominance hormone, testosterone, but is sometimes seen in older dogs of a submissive or fearful nature, and so there is a chance it could affect the older inherited pet.

It is a response to what the dog perceives as demonstration of dominance by some member of the family, a stranger or another animal. It can be a component of the over-excitement urination on meeting (see page 129) where, for instance, the dog has conflicting emotions, happy to see the person but perhaps at the same time mindful of punishment he recently received for some misdemeanour. He may interpret certain movements, gestures, facial expressions or the volume or tone of voice as being potentially menacing. He adopts the typical posture of submission with low body posture, flattening of the ears against the head, evasion of eye contact, etc. in order to signal meek acceptance of the situation in the hope of preventing the threat developing further. Urination is just part of the subordinate individual's show of 'creeping' to his superiors.

At the start of his life a young puppy is accustomed to being turned over and thoroughly licked by his mother. The licking stimulates him to urinate and also cleans away the urine (and any faecal matter). Certainly by about three weeks of age he recognizes that 'upside down' means time to pee. But 'upside down' is a submissive position and Mum is acting in a dominant role. So it seems that some dogs carry the idea of submission and urination into later life.

Treatment

The essential point in managing your dog if he is prone to submissive urination is the need to increase the dog's confidence and self-esteem. Punishment and displays of apparent dominance by family members must be avoided. Do not scold and never intimidate him in any way. He should be praised for doing the right thing and for not doing the wrong thing. Use a phrase like 'Good boy' or Good girl' regularly when petting and feeding him and then go on to say those words whenever he does something commendable like sitting waiting for food or fetching a toy instead of urinating when you enter the house.

When meeting the dog both you and your visitors should at first ignore him (very important if he has started to pee) and then, when he eventually approaches you (not the other way round), talk to him quietly. Too much fussy attention too early can reinforce the unwanted behaviour. It is often a good idea to give him a toy, a food treat, or a few moments' play at this point thereby implanting the idea that meetings are good times, free of uncertainty. Avoid looming over the dog – crouch or kneel down when petting him and always pat him from underneath his muzzle, chest or stomach with the palm of your hand held upwards. It is worth repeating yet again: simple obedience training can be invaluable in tackling this problem successfully.

Kneeling down at the dog's level and patting it from underneath gives confidence to a submissively urinating dog.

THE UN-HOUSE-TRAINED DOG

You could be unlucky and find that the dog you have acquired is not house-trained or only uncertainly so. Although this is less likely to be the case with an old dog, it sometimes happens. Assuming that you are sure that other causes such as separation anxiety or medical problems are not involved, how do you go about the basics of educating or re-educating him?

House-training

Here are the guidelines to successful house-training. You should start as soon as the dog arrives in his new home.

1 When you bring the pet home for the first time, give him the opportunity to relieve himself immediately. Take him outside as often as possible and keep him under supervision – don't just let him out and close the door on him. You must go too and praise him when he does what is required.

2 If access to a garden is easy, take him outside whenever he wakes up from a sleep, after meals, drinks or an excited game-playing session, and if he hasn't urinated for some time or is showing signs of wishing to do so. Stay outside long enough for him to urinate and/or defecate. Let the pup walk out with you rather than carry him, since he will then recognize the route and learn to go to the door when he needs to go out. Until he is able to go through the night without accidents, put newspaper by the door at night – you will soon be able to discard it.

3 Do not punish 'mistakes'. Instead, praise him when he gets it right. If you catch him in the act of urinating indoors interrupt the behaviour by sharply clapping your hands and saying 'No!' fairly loudly. Take him outside at once and thoroughly clean and de-odorize the soiled area inside the house.

4 If he has to be left alone for long periods, consider asking a neighbour to visit occasionally or confine him to a small area close to his bed (dogs are usually averse to urinating or defecating there) or, particularly if you live in a flat, try newspaper training. The aim is to teach the dog to relieve himself on newspaper, until you place it outside. Confine your dog to an easily cleaned room and cover the floor with newspaper. When he develops a preference for one area, remove the paper from the rest of the floor. Then you gradually move the 'toilet' paper until eventually it is placed by the door. On a fine day, place the paper outside. The next day remove the paper altogether. Hopefully the pet will subsequently relieve himself outside.

Older dogs can be toilet-trained in the same way as puppies using newspaper.

1 House-train the dog exactly as if he were a puppy using the methods outlined above. A dog cannot be considered house-trained until he has gone for at least six consecutive weeks without soiling in the home.

2 Take him outside often and give rewards of praise and food titbits when he performs correctly. Do not offer food treats at any other time.

3 Thoroughly cleaning and de-odorizing any soiled places is even more important when dealing with older dogs.

4 Bear in mind that an old dog that has been house-soiling for many years with a previous owner will often take many months to be trained to a dependable level.

Be patient and don't get frustrated or angry if it takes time to house-train your new pet.

Praise him when he does so. Keep an eye out for warning signs, including him looking for his paper near the doorway.

UNWELCOME DEFECATION

House soiling by faeces is much more commonly done by bitches rather than male dogs, and many of the causes of dogs depositing stools inside the house are the same as for unwelcome urination. Old dogs require access to outdoors more often than younger ones and ailments such as arthritis have to be considered. Other medical problems that may result in faecal soiling and require veterinary treatment include: diarrhoea, colitis, malabsorption and maldigestion conditions, some forms of neurological disease and, of course, cognitive dysfunction in the elderly. Too much fibre in a dog's diet or some kind of food that is badly tolerated can also cause it, as can sudden changes in the diet or feeding schedule. Some dogs defecate to mark their property or territory, the faeces carrying chemical messages produced by the anal gland secretions that can be 'read' by other dogs that come a-sniffing.

Feeding too close to bedtime or to the time when you leave for work, leaving the dog alone, and fear of going outside due to a recent unpleasant experience (inclement weather, particularly thunder and lightning storms, or mistreatment by a neighbour) are other possible causes. Always check that your dog did indeed pass urine and stools when he was outside before allowing him back in.

Treatment

Correcting this kind of behaviour is usually not difficult and involves taking the same measures as outlined above for dealing with unwelcome urination. You may need to change your dog's diet and also ensure that feeding times are regular and on schedule. If it appears to be a case of the pet not having been house-trained fully or at all, then you should begin house-training him immediately.

OLD DOG NEW TRICKS

*Fear him who fears thee,
though he be a fly and thou an elephant.*
SADI, THE THIRTEENTH-CENTURY PERSIAN POET.

FEARFUL AND PHOBIC DOGS

10

Some dogs exhibit a variety of anxious and fearful behaviours for a wide range of reasons. The most common ones are explored in this chapter. I suppose the wild canids are afflicted by only one phobia, that of *Homo sapiens* in the form of farmers, shepherds, trappers and, of course, the sort that Oscar Wilde called 'the unspeakable in full pursuit of the uneatable'. The fears and phobias (unreasonable fears) of dogs are, however, like those of people, many and various. They can be classified into five main sorts: fear of people including children; fear of places; fear of animals; fear of noises; and separation anxiety. Your newly acquired pet could, unknown at first to you, be troubled by any of them. Separation anxiety is the most likely, especially if he is an old dog.

TYPES OF FEAR

Fear, the reaction to disturbing stimuli, has three principal elements, at least in the human being. Firstly there are physiological effects which automatically and involuntarily gear up the frightened individual for flight or fight. Dilation of the pupils to widen the field of vision, the increased output of blood from the heart, the surge of glucose into the blood to provide instant extra energy for action – these and other changes in the body are largely as a result of nervous commands from the brain instructing the adrenal glands to pour out lots of the hormone adrenalin. This also occurs in dogs.

Then there is behavioural change designed to either neutralize the stimulus or to escape from it. Both man and dog exhibit this. Through their behaviour they can either show that they are willing to submit to the threat, stand and fight, or try to make a run for it. It is impossible to say whether the third component of fear in humans, the effect on the emotions, is also present in dogs.

Some dogs are more prone to fearfulness than others, and there does seem to be a genetic factor. Labradors, for example, are worse than most other breeds for displaying fear of noises. Individual temperament, of course, plays a part, but undoubtedly the biggest factor in a fearful dog's make-up is the environmental and experiential one: how he has been treated and what he has encountered since he was born. In addition, other things that occur at the same time as something unpleasant is happening to a dog may, in the future, act as a stimuli that triggers the fearful reaction. If a factory hooter goes off at the moment the animal is being, say, beaten, the sound of the hooter alone may thereafter result in signs of fear.

Treating fears and phobias is not difficult if the dog was not deprived of socialization experience during the first months of life and if the problem developed as an adult. It is not easy if the animal has displayed fearful responses since puppy-hood and especially, as is sometimes the case, if there was and is no apparent reason for the fear, and no traumatic incident involving the feared stimulus during its upbringing. For all types of fear and phobia, before employing appropriate treatment stratagems, it is a basic requirement that the dog is trained to obediently sit when commanded and to follow dependably at heel when in the home and his owner is moving about. (Any tendency to lead the owner must be corrected by giving a signal – a clap of the hand is ideal – and at once reversing the direction of movement.)

SEPARATION ANXIETY

A number of behaviour problems, most frequently destructiveness and excessive noise-making, have separation anxiety as one of the possible causes. Anxiety is to be expected in a fairly high percentage of 'inherited' dogs, particularly old ones. Similar attacks of anxiety are commonplace in elderly people whose lives have been drastically altered, perhaps by a bereavement or having to move from the home they have lived in for decades. For a dog, the sudden death or hospitalization of an owner or another dog in the household can be a profoundly unsettling event. The mental processes of both old dogs and elderly human beings are less tolerant of and adaptable to change than those of younger individuals.

Loneliness is a common ingredient of the condition. Being left alone for extended periods of time will induce it, as will the long-lasting effects of inadequate opportunities to socialize with fellow animals or human beings in the early months of life. Frightening experiences, such as thunderstorms, physical punishment or being alone when a neighbour objects to the dog's barking or howling by hammering on the wall or yelling through the letterbox, may be involved. Human beings may unintentionally reinforce the anxiety, as when an owner, hearing the dog howl after the door is closed on leaving the house, then returns to console him. Hearing sounds, such as voices, footsteps or cars pulling up outside which are not then followed by the hoped-for entry of the owner into the house, can create anxiety in the dog.

Treatment

This entails avoiding problematic situations, correcting your own behaviour patterns if necessary, and using a crate, kennel, run, dog-proof room or playpen to confine the dog when you are absent. However, it is important that the dog recognizes the containing space as his own private den, not as a prison (see page 55). If advised by the vet, anxiolytic (anxiety-relieving) medication may also be necessary. Alternative medicine, in the form of flower essences containing extracts of such plants as red chestnut, mimulus, impatiens and aspen, has also proved very effective in reducing anxiety in dogs. These products can be obtained from herbalists or on the internet. Often, for a lonely animal, acquiring a second pet is the ideal therapeutic solution.

There does seem to be a virtue in leaving a radio on, tuned to a classical music station, when a dog is left alone. Recently it has been shown that music by such masters as Mozart, Haydn and Bach does have a relaxing, calming effect on Labrador Retrievers. Music from a CD player or radio may help mask certain troubling noises.

FEAR OF PEOPLE

A dog's behaviour when he is in the presence of a person he fears will be in one of the three forms mentioned earlier: submissive, aggressive or taking flight. Some are fearful of any stranger, others react only to certain types of folk, postmen and/or anyone in uniform, men with facial hair, women with umbrellas, people of a different skin colour to their owners, babies, old folk who walk 'oddly' with the aid of a stick or Zimmer frame, etc. I mustn't forget to mention the sort in white coats smelling of antiseptic who generally seem to be carrying sharp objects in their hands and are commonly called vets.

Treatment

First identify the problem. Is it all old people or just those carrying sticks? (I remember a case where it was the walking stick alone that was the cause of great fear reaction in a Scottie, which had been considered initially to be an exponent of canine ageism. It turned out she had been hit regularly with one by a previous owner.) Determine roughly at what distance from the stimulus the dog begins to display signs of fear.

Next, with the dog under your full control, preferably on a halter and lead, start at a distance where he can see the stimulus but is not showing signs of apprehension. Tell him to sit and give him a food reward. Gradually decrease the distance, stopping at intervals, commanding the 'Sit' position and rewarding him. This cannot be achieved in one session; it may take many exposures to the stimulus over some days.

If uniforms are the problem, go through the process with a variety of people who wear them: commissionaires, postmen, policemen, etc. A dog fearful of babies can be introduced at first to older children and then accustomed to the scents and sounds of an infant. Let him smell the baby's pillow and listen to a recording of typical cries. For more on introducing your newly arrived dog to babies and vice versa see page 26.

NOTE: Punishment must never be used for this or any other kind of phobia.

The introduction of dog to infant requires careful handling and the use of a lead at first.

EXCESSIVE SHYNESS/SUBMISSIVENESS

Shyness and submissiveness are not entirely synonymous. Wild dogs, wolves and most other non-domesticated animals are naturally shy of human beings and no wonder. Submissiveness is a behavioural technique, which, as we discussed earlier, is employed to avoid conflict and signify acceptance of a subordinate status. The typical features of submissiveness, the behaviour, body postures and facial expressions, have already been described. Nearly all cases of excessive submissiveness are to be found in dogs less than nine years of age. Often dogs that are described by their owners as 'shy' are, in fact, overly submissive as a result of repeated bouts of punishment. As is, sadly, only too well known with abused children and women, these animals lose all their self-confidence.

Treatment

If you have inherited such a dog you must understand that punishment of any kind, physical, threatening or scolding, is taboo. If, at the same time, the over-submissive dog exhibits other behavioural faults, of the types described earlier, they must be corrected in ways avoiding punishment. Never loom over your dog when you are both engaged in therapy sessions or, indeed at any other time, but rather crouch down or kneel when interacting with him.

Begin simple obedience training, rewarding the basic commands of 'Come', 'Sit' and 'Stay', even if they are only imperfectly responded to, with praise and, when the dog is within reach, gentle petting. Be careful when touching him, and do not use force to make him sit or to restrain him. Pet him from underneath on the underside of the muzzle, chest and abdomen, not downwards onto the top of the head. He may well have been accustomed to slaps delivered there in the past. If hand-shy, it may be best to begin touching the dog with a stuffed glove on a stick, building up its tolerance gradually. Then first offer a fist rather than fingers (to avoid getting bitten by a highly-strung individual whose warning signs you may have missed.)

When strangers call it is important to ignore any negative reactions displayed by the dog such as urinating, running off or whining, while praising him lavishly whenever he shows courage and confidence. Because the dog will pick up any signs of tension or exasperation on your part, you must be relaxed and affable at such times, laughing, smiling and talking as if it is not serious.

Make sure that younger members of the family know to take care when stroking overly shy animals.

SUBMISSION IN WILD CANIDS

I have never seen excessive submissiveness displayed by wild canids, undoubtedly because they are not subject to repeated punishment at the hand of man. Submissive behaviour on their part is, however, quite frequent. One of my favourite wild relatives of our domestic pet, the African Hunting Dog, has a range of submissive behaviours which I have been privileged to witness from time to time in East Africa. Sometimes, when a dog higher in the hierarchy approaches, it will behave rather like a cub being cleaned by its mother – rolling onto its back, tail forwards between the hind legs, and ears laid back. Alternatively, it may crouch, with tail carried low and even wagging, and then attempt to nuzzle and lick at the muzzle of its superior.

Another submissive signal, also often given by the Golden Jackal, is to turn away the head, thus presenting the side of the neck towards the other animal, much like the winsome movement of a young lady in a Jane Austen novel. Most surprising of all is the way in which some adult male hunting dogs will creep under the belly of the oldest female in the pack and lick her teats, a highly submissive behaviour recalling their days of puppyhood.

It is generally thought that this behaviour derives from the infantile way of begging for food and is intended to evoke benign, parental-type responses rather than those which would normally be directed towards an adult. Both of these forms of submissive behaviour can be seen in domestic dogs and have been observed in many other wild Canids.

FEAR OF PLACES

First identify what it is about a specific place that stimulates a fearful response in your dog. Is it the area in general or perhaps certain visible aspects, smells or sounds within it? It is important to establish this if you are to treat the condition successfully.

Treatment

It may be possible to avoid visiting such places permanently. If not, you should certainly keep the dog away from them when you are not on an actual desensitizing, training session.

As with people phobia, start at a distance from the problem site. Use the 'Sit' command and reward the dog generously for compliant behaviour. Gradually, over several sessions, bring him closer, always stopping just before he is likely to become

1 If your dog is visibly frightened when approaching a place or another animal, command 'Sit'.

2 By distracting your dog with food treats, his attention will be diverted from the fear stimulus.

3 Reward your dog for compliant behaviour, and when he seems to visibly relax.

apprehensive. Adopt a happy, calming tone of voice together with giving a reward. If you misjudge the distance and your dog does begin to show signs of anxiety, ignore him and withdraw or, if he calms down quickly or you can draw his attention elsewhere, praise him immediately, pat him and offer a food reward. For the next session don't get quite so close at first. Another method is to put down a trail of rewards into the place where the dog shows signs of fear. If there are at least two escape routes and you have the animal on a long lead this may distract it.

FEAR OF ANIMALS

As always, you need to identify the exact nature of the dog's fearfulness. Is it only big dogs, or little ones that dart about, or dogs that dash in to make acquaintance up close and personal? Is your dog only frightened when he is out for walks, but not when in your garden? Try to determine what the minimum distance is between your dog and the problem animal before fearfulness is displayed.

Treatment

As with the two previously described types of phobia, treatment begins with the dog under your full halter/lead control at a distance that does not elicit fear of the stimulus. If possible, the first sessions should be on home territory such as your garden. Gradually shorten the distance, stopping to give 'Sit' commands and praise and food rewards on compliance. The emphasis must be on 'gradually'. Do not rush things. Several, perhaps many, sessions may be needed and each time the distance between the dogs should be slightly reduced.

If big dogs are the problem, arrange desensitization sessions using at first small animals, then medium-sized and finally big ones. As treatment progresses, change the venue for the sessions by, say, going to the park or a neighbour's garden, and introduce a variety of shapes and styles of dog breed – pedigree or mongrel, it makes no difference.

FEAR OF NOISES

This common fear can be due to a variety of sharp, loud noises, most commonly thunder, gunshots and fireworks. It is impossible to go through a series of desensitizing training sessions for thunderstorms, and impractical, except for police and army dogs, in the case of fireworks and other explosions.

Treatment

You can use the method of gradually decreasing the distance between the affected dog and the stimulus which has been outlined in chapter 7, together with praise and reward for non-fearful behaviour. If possible, the noise stimulus should at first be at a low level. This is not always easy to arrange and distance alone may be the only way of graduating the sound volume. Obedience to the 'Sit' command is vital. If the dog does show fear he should be ignored or distracted in some way. When he settles down, praise, petting and a food reward must be instantly forth-coming. Some people recommend the use of a CD entitled, 'Fear of Fireworks', containing all the noises of rockets, bangers, Roman candles and the like at varying intensities. It should only be used as recommended in training dogs by gradual desensitization to lose their fear in the way described above for other unpleasant stimuli. It is now available from some veterinary practices and on the internet.

For fireworks on bonfire night or at other festival times, tranquillizers such as Valium and acepromazine should be obtained from your vet and given in good time before the fun begins. At such times, always keep your dog inside the house, and if he is accustomed to the soothing strains of classical music on the radio he will appreciate, and often be visibly calmed by, a CD playing.

Recently melatonin, the drug now widely used for jet lag and sleep disturbance in humans, has been suggested as a useful therapeutic for noise-phobic dogs. In the bodies of both man and other animals, melatonin, a hormone involved with inducing sleep, is produced naturally by the pineal gland in the brain. More work needs to be done on this but, if you are interested in trying it, discuss it with your vet.

A diffuser spray that plugs into an electric socket and emits DAP, a chemical mimicking the pheromones indicating well-being and appeasement, that are present in a bitch's urine, has a calming effect on dogs, and so can prove useful in noise phobia and other stress-related cases.

Some dogs that are frightened of loud noises have hearing problems of a medical nature; their hearing may be hyper-sensitive or, yes it's true, rather poor. The latter condition may make them jump at a sudden loud noise. A veterinary examination is needed in such cases and treatment is often possible. It is most important that owners do not become irritated when a dog is afraid and that they do not fuss over, baby-talk and cuddle the pet. Fussing can be mistaken for praise, thereby reinforcing the displays of fear.

FEAR OF WATER

Some dogs, even Labrador Retrievers, are innately frightened of water. Especially if you live near the sea, a river or lake, it is wise to change your pet's attitude by teaching him to swim as well as being fun for you both. This must never be by simply chucking the animal into the water, shallow or deep, like a sack of potatoes – that will only increase his fear.

Treatment

The following method will work with both puppies and old, inherited dogs. It is best done in calm weather and water conditions by two people, one of whom stays on the shore while the other, the owner, goes into the water up to about knee depth. Take the dog into the water supporting his body with your arms under his belly. When you are some three to five yards out, lower him slowly into the water making sure to keep him at all times level. The dog will automatically start to paddle with his forepaws. Yes, it's learning the 'dog paddle'. At first keep your support under his belly and give lots of verbal encouragement and praise. Have the dog in a position facing the shore. Gradually drop your supporting arms while your companion on shore calls the dog, again with congratulatory words and an encouraging tone of voice. If the dog's rear starts to sink, push it up – it must stay level. The dog will normally continue paddling back to land with you accompanying him closely. On arrival give him abundant praise and rewards of petting and treats. Try to arrange sessions of this on a daily basis and, as the dog gains confidence, introduce simple retrieving by throwing a stick or ball a short distance in front of the swimming animal.

You never know, your dog could take like a duck to the water and even rival Jake, a Golden Retriever who in August 2005 swam from the prison island of Alcatraz to the San Francisco shore in 42 minutes. The only non-human entrant among 500 swimmers in the competition, he came seventy-second, the first dog ever recorded to have made the crossing. No hydrophobia there!

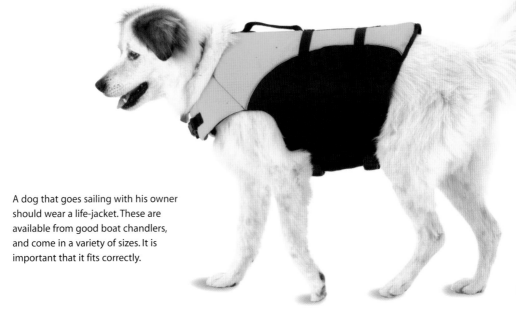

A dog that goes sailing with his owner should wear a life-jacket. These are available from good boat chandlers, and come in a variety of sizes. It is important that it fits correctly.

COMPULSIVE OR STEREOTYPICAL DISORDERS

Compulsive behaviours are those where a dog has no control over starting or stopping them. However, where they seem to have no obvious goal or value they are sometimes termed stereotypical. Obsessive licking of a leg can be so intense in some cases that first the hair and then the skin and underlying flesh are removed, even down to the bone. The licked area is constantly weeping and becomes chronically inflamed. The wound tries to heal producing 'proud flesh', which is in turn licked away. This condition of acral lick dermatitis rarely clears up spontaneously without veterinary treatment. The cause can be purely some form of localized pathology but in the majority of cases stress of some sort in the dog's life or environment is again involved.

Treatment

Treatment, after careful clinical examination usually with laboratory tests and X-rays to rule out other conditions and determine the extent of the damage, consists of both medical treatment which will consist of such things as anti-inflammatory, antibiotic, anti-depressant medication and protective dressing of the affected area to fend off the abrasive tongue. Behaviour modification is equally important and can be done by identifying the underlying stimuli producing the stress or anxiety, and then employing the training techniques described for self-mutilation (see page 146) and destructiveness (see page 122) as well as obedience to simple commands, distraction and reward for compliance.

In addition, it is essential to give your dog plenty of exercise and play time, and to make his life more interesting and colourful by providing a variety of toys, objects he can investigate and chew into bits like cardboard boxes and, especially if he is left alone during the day, to consider obtaining a second pet or arranging for a friend to visit and take him out while you are absent. Elizabethan collars to deny access to the affected area are very effective, while applying hopefully deterrent bitter or 'hot' sprays or creams will work in some cases, but in others serve only to intensify the licking impulse still further.

A similar condition, to which Dobermann Pinschers appear particularly prone and seems to be hereditary in certain bloodlines, is flank sucking, where the dog compulsively suckles an area of its flank skin. In only a few cases is the damage inflicted severe enough to break the skin and create inflamed, weeping ulcers. Stress of some sort is probably the cause and the management of such cases should be as for acral dermatitis.

As well as self-mutilation, other compulsive disorders can be seen sometimes in dogs, among them circling, pacing, tail-chasing and snapping at imaginary flies. They can be tackled in the same way by simple training. Only a few, intractable cases might need the prescription of anti-anxiety or anti-depressant drugs by a veterinarian.

In all cases of tail chasing veterinary examination of the dog is advisable in case there is an underlying physical condition of the anal glands, spine or hip joints involved.

TAIL CHASING

Tail chasing is a behaviour frequently seen from time to time in puppies and if occurring only at times of excitement and not lasting long, it can be disregarded. In some dogs, however, it can be a persistent, debilitating obsession affecting even middle-aged animals. Only a very few old dogs suffer from it. It is more commonly found in certain breeds, such as the Bull Terrier and German Shepherd, and in the former it is the commonest compulsive disorder brought to the attention of vets and dog psychologists.

Symptoms

The affected dog may circle fairly slowly with his attention fixed on his tail or, particularly in Bull Terriers, he may spin rapidly like a top without focusing on the tail itself. The animal may indulge in both these forms of chasing or 'specialize' in just one, and the frequency and intensity of tail chasing bouts may steadily increase as time passes. Some dogs just start doing it without any apparent trigger stimulus, while with others some form of stress in their psychological state or environment that is fuelling anxiety, can be identified. Owners playing with puppies and encouraging their pet to twirl can initiate the problem and reinforce its recurrence, but the true cause of some severe tail chasing cases is unknown.

Treatment

When correcting tail chasing, it is necessary first to make sure that there is no physical cause such as a painful sore, buried thorn or itchy patch of dermatitis under the fur anywhere on the tail that might be the cause. Any identifiable trigger source or cause of anxiety should be avoided or remedied.

No attention to the behaviour, which might reinforce it, other than remedial interruption or distraction, must be given. You can try to interrupt and/or distract your dog when he is chasing and then use the obedience training commands we have talked so much about, perhaps in combination with a lead and halter at the same time If the owner was responsible in the first place for initiating or reinforcing the behaviour this may work, but in many other cases the tail chasing will continue. For these dogs, veterinary medication by means of anti-anxiety drugs, anti-depressives or sedatives may be necessary.

SELF-MUTILATION

The dog that seems to lick or gnaw obsessively at parts of his own body can, in some cases, progress to inflict significant damage to his skin. Naturally, the first thing to eliminate in such cases is the possibility that the cause is a persistent itch or irritation caused by some form of parasite or physical ailment. Veterinary examination is required to look for, and if necessary treat, such things as flea or tick infestation or allergic skin disease, the latter triggered perhaps by something in the dog's diet or in environment (sleeping on straw, rolling on a lawn recently treated with weed killer, etc). You may think your dog is free of fleas but frequently, somewhere in his coat, just one, single, tiny, lonely flea can cause a troublesome itchy allergic response when it inserts its mouthparts into the dog's skin. Assuming there are neither fleas nor any other physical cause, what might be the cause of this obsession?

Treatment

Simple training can usually put matters right. No need for leads and halters – the key is establishing a solid owner-dog relationship. Basic obedience training is called for with praise and petting being withheld until and unless the dog responds promptly to commands. When the dog self-mutilates with the owner present, he must be distracted immediately – by throwing a ball, a loud clap of the hands, a whistle, the rattle of a tin can – then given a command – 'Sit', 'Come' or 'Stay' – and a reward of praise, fondling and a food titbit when he complies.

It is more difficult if the self-mutilation only tends to occur when the owner is absent. In that case it is necessary to spy unseen upon the dog and distract him by arranging for a tin can to fall when a string is pulled or, more sophisticatedly, by means of a remote control training collar. If a dog is self-mutilating because of stress do not employ the whistle or loud noise if it causes anxiety. Also, if such a sound signal produces no response, it is best to use a positive distraction instead.

CASE HISTORY: OBSESSIVE BEHAVIOUR

Bouncer was a 10-year-old male Beagle whose owner had died suddenly and was subsequently inherited by a client of mine. A few days after he arrived in his new home Bouncer began chewing at his right forepaw. The new owner washed the paw, couldn't see anything obviously wrong with it, but smeared on a little antiseptic cream. Bouncer didn't stop chewing the paw. It was covered with a child's sock but Bouncer chewed through the sock and continued gnawing his paw, which was now almost hairless on the top surface. The Beagle was brought to surgery. With nothing significant to be found in the paw, I decided to try some corticosteroid ointment rubbed well in twice a day but Bouncer kept chewing and the paw began to bleed. In places it became ulcerated but still Bouncer chewed on. Ultimately I came to the conclusion that the dog's self-mutilation was, as is so often the case, a manifestation of stress, in his case the effects of the disappearance of a much loved, long-time owner, and his move to a strange, new, albeit caring, family.

A dog behaviourist was called in and each day she spent an hour with the owner and dog. After only three days of appointments Bouncer had lost all interest in gnawing the paw. Cases such as Bouncer's are not rare, but it's not always as easy to identify as in his case what is causing the stress or frustration that lies at their roots. If the cause is correctable, so well and good, but often it isn't.

With all forms of fear and phobia in dogs, owners should endeavour to reduce stress on the animal by employing thoughtful management and consistent, gentle but firm handling within a peaceful environment. Chewing marrow bones or cow-hide chews helps to reduce an animal's stress, and some herbal preparations, including ones that contain Skullcap (Scutellaria laterifolia) and Passion flower (Passiflora incarnata), are available that, in my experience, can prove effective aids in treating many 'nervy' pet dogs.

It cannot be stressed enough that prevention is always the best cure and, if you are in a position to be able to give your dog the training before he develops behaviour problems then you are well on the way to a long and happy relationship with your dog. Of course, this is not always the case – particularly with rescued or rehomed dogs, in which cases simple obedience training can go a long way to improving your dog's wellbeing.

Certain anxious dogs seem to calm visibly when their ears are stroked. Always approach the dog from the front and under the muzzle.

They grin like a dog, and run about through the city.

EXCITABLE UNRULY DOGS

11

If your newly acquired dog is over nine years of age it is unlikely that he will prove to be unruly and hyper-excitable. Unruliness comes in various forms, and the term can be applied to some of the undesirable behaviours we have already discussed. All of them have, as a common ingredient, lack of control by the owner. Obedience training with the use of a lead and halter, when appropriate, is essential in all cases.

HYPERACTIVITY AND OVER-EXCITABILITY

Dogs may have a predisposition to hyperactivity in their genetic makeup, and it tends to affect young animals in particular. The passing of time tends to calm down their behaviour automatically. There are many possible reasons: some simply do not get enough exercise, whereas others have been inadvertently reinforced in their behaviour by their owner's actions.

Symptoms

Some dogs become very excited only when they are in certain specific situations, charging around and barking persistently – Poodles are rather prone to act in this way. Our Westie used to do it when he went with my mother into the cellar at home and she switched on the light. He would dash up and down the cellar steps, staring at one wall fixedly and making lots of noise. Mum always claimed he was 'chasing the electricity'! What she should have done, instead of talking to him about 'what a silly boy he was, the electricity would do him no harm, they'd be upstairs in a minute and she'd give him a barley sugar' and so forth, thereby reinforcing what was essentially attention-seeking behaviour, was to ignore him completely and give a reward only if and when he settled down and became calm. Or, better still, not have taken him into the cellar at all; he wasn't much use helping her with the washing she did down there, anyway!

Treatment

Correcting the condition involves giving a hyperactive dog lots of regular exercise and playtime to burn off excess energy. Obedience training sessions are essential and are best undertaken after exercise. Always train your dog in a variety of environments and give rewards for calm responses to commands. Rewards should only be for calmness and quiet behaviour, and you should ignore any attempts by your dog to gain attention, initiate play or obtain some form of reward on his own initiative, especially when he exhibits 'pushiness'. A halter and long lead are the key items of training equipment. Never resort to physical punishment; instead, distract the excited dog by means of some type of sharp sound or a remote control collar (see page 128).

Drugs from the vet are rarely indicated, but mild tranquillizers may be indicated in the early stages of training in a few severe cases. In almost all cases, they are prescribed in tablet form, but injectable forms, such as Valium and acepromazine are used in particular cases, very rarely, though, for this condition.

JUMPING UP AT PEOPLE

This annoying habit is often the result of inconsistent behaviour by members of the family. It is a natural reaction for people to respond to an effusive greeting in similar vein. With a jumping-up dog this can significantly reinforce the behaviour. All family members and friends must be told not to reward the dog by fussing over him, and praising or petting him in return. Keep all meetings undemonstrative and very much on the cool side.

Treatment

Obedience training is important to ensure that the dog responds to commands of 'Sit' and 'Stay'. A reward of praise, calmly delivered, should be given when the dog greets someone without jumping up. Punishment must be limited to a sharp 'No!' accompanied perhaps, at first, by a sharp sound signal or a squirt from a water pistol. Distraction can be used (see page 108) followed by a command to do something, which is then rewarded by praise, petting or a titbit when the dog complies promptly and correctly. Again, at least in the early stages of training, a long lead and halter are recommended.

Two other ways of tackling jumping up are also worth mentioning. One is to crouch down on your haunches when the dog runs to greet you. (Tricky, I admit, for Grandma!) The reason for this is that there is no need for him to jump up when your face is more or less on a level with his.

Crouching down when greeting your dog, can help prevent him jumping up to meet you. This is particularly important where big dogs and small children are concerned.

After using this method for some time you can try reverting to standing up at greeting time. Some dogs will lose the bad habit; others will simply go back to jumping up.

The other method is to simply ignore your dog when he jumps up. If you like you can designate an area in the house that is dedicated to fussing and praise, and walk straight to that place when your dog jumps, where your dog can expect cuddles. If you train every member of the household to do this, the dog may even preempt you, running straight to this 'fuss-mat', as soon as you come through the door! Of course very big dogs or ones with arthriticky joints tend not to be keen 'jumpers up'.

1 A dog who jumps up can be ignored if he is proving over-zealous at the front door when visitors arrrive. No fuss or praise should be given at the entrance, to the persistent jumper.

2 Folding your arms and turning away, can be an immediate solution to the slobbering and licking of hands.

GENERAL UNRULY BEHAVIOUR

Some dogs, like some young people, treat their home in a rather undisciplined manner. Working surfaces or tables are jumped upon, things are chewed, waste bins are rooted through or items, often including foodstuffs, are stolen. Unlike young people, however, dogs have no concept of right or wrong when they behave in this way. It's fun, it's interesting, and it obtains for them something they fancy. They do know, however, that their owner will intervene, often even punish them to some degree, if they witness this behaviour.

Treatment

The management of this kind of unruliness is not difficult and is largely common sense. Once again it is important to train your pet in basic obedience to commands and to provide adequate regular exercise and play time. By maintaining control of your dog and asserting your leadership, you are insisting that he shows you respect, something dogs that steal or vandalize, particularly in the presence of family members, often lack. Grabbing hold of an object that the dog is carrying off as booty usually results in a tug o' war, and should be avoided. Such a 'game', as the dog perceives it, serves only to reinforce the undesirable behaviour. Interrupt acts of canine pilfering with distractions and obedience commands, rewarding immediate compliance in the usual manner. There should be no physical punishment of any kind.

Deny your dog access to certain target areas of the house where possible, and don't leave uncovered food items within his reach. If the problem occurs only when you are out at work, consider confining the dog to a crate (see page 54) or kennel that is comfortable, not too small, and equipped with food and water facilities and a favourite toy or two. He should be taught to regard the container, not as a prison, but as his own, snug den, which he will enter on command. Toys and other objects that are rightly his property can be smeared with something he likes such as a little cream cheese or meat paste. Objects that he must stop interfering with should be anointed with hot pepper sauce or sprayed with one of the deterrent preparations available from the vet or pet shop. Each day move the objects around the house and each week apply the deterrent substance to some other item. A deterrent in the form of an automatically conrolled electronic alarm can be useful in some situations, but they should never be harmful.

It is vital to reinforce good behaviour by rewarding your dog with praise, petting or titbits whenever he plays with his own toys and chews on his own items of property.

RUNNING AWAY

Obviously no dog, certainly not your newly 'inherited' one, should be permitted to wander off from the home territory. Freely wandering animals are at risk of disease, injury and death in so many ways. Some dogs that can get out and about by jumping over or digging under fences or even have the back gate opened for them by a foolish owner on demand, have a regular itinerary in the neighbourhood, with habitual stopping places where they eat or socialize. A dog newly arrived in the family has been known to try to return to his previous home and owner, sometimes with success and over enormous distances.

'I'll just pop out for a while and pay a visit to that attractive little Pug down the road.'

TRAVELLING DOGS

Bear, a seven-year-old Labrador/Chow cross, disappeared from his home in Wichita, USA, in November 1997 and only came back, apparently none the worse for wear, two days before Thanksgiving in 2003. Another seasoned canine traveller was Archie, a Labrador who, after being separated from his owner at the railway station in Inverurie, Scotland, found his way home, naturally by train.

Dogs that regularly go off on walk-about are clearly missing something at home. Usually the fault lies with the owners, either by allowing their pet to become too dependent upon them or because they are not perceived by the dog as dominant leaders in the family packs.

Treatment

Correcting the bad habit means, of course, taking steps to close off all possible exit points from the home property and instilling obedience through basic training. The 'Sit', 'Stay' and 'Come' commands must be responded to reliably so that you are seen very much as 'the boss' by your dog. When he shows signs of 'pushiness', importuning food, fondling or opening a door by means of nudges and pawing, ignore him, then give a command and reward him with a quick bout of praise and petting when he obeys. Consistency on your part in handling him in this way will soon see a new relationship forged between the two of you, with the dog respectful and deferential but not over-dependent, and happy to stay at home until you decide it's time for exercise or a play session in the park. Make sure that coming home is as much fun as going there by means of interactive toys and chews as well as fulsome praise.

Accidents can happen, of course, and even a well-trained dog might one day get lost when off the lead. Collars with identity discs and micro-chips inserted under the skin by a vet are essential for all dogs, not just newly inherited ones. And you'll need the micro-chip together with his pet passport when you both pop off for the weekend to your gîte in Normandy!

Make sure that your dog is happy to return home, if necessary by giving cuddles and saying 'Good boy or girl'.

Like wolves, each dog has its own individual voice, which can be distinguished by its fellows.

NOISY DOGS

Wild members of the canid family make use of loud sounds to communicate over long distances; the best-known example of this is the howling of wolves. Howling maintains contact between members of a pack and is often choral in nature, with one beginning to howl, then all the others joining in and the concert continuing often for some considerable time. The sound apparently has a bonding effect, and scientists studying wolves have found that they could cement friendships with the wild animals far more quickly if they also took part in the chorus.

Each domestic dog, like its cousins, the wolf and the fox, has its own individual voice, with personal characteristics that can come to be recognized by others of their kind. For wolves and hyenas particularly, the vocal sounds help locate friends and deter strangers. The fox's bark is probably purely intended to warn off intruders.

Long-distance conversations may be fine for wild canids, but noisy domestic dogs can be a cause of considerable friction with neighbours, especially if you live in an apartment. Certain breeds of dog tend to be very noisy, especially terriers, some toy dogs, many of the working breeds, Beagles, Collies, Norwegian Elkhounds, American Eskimo dogs and the Finnish Spitz.

Why do pet dogs bark?

Pet dogs bark, howl, yowl or whine for one of around half a dozen reasons: to announce their presence, to answer another dog's vocalization or to stimulate another dog to vocalize (a sort of 'Anybody out there?' call), to warn that they are in defensive mode and may go on to attack, to alert the family pack to some perceived threat (like Postman Pat ringing the doorbell) or to inform them that a potential prey animal has been sighted (a cat, squirrel, etc.), to warn outsiders that they are intruding into their territory (Postman Pat again), and to seek relief from some unpleasant or frustrating situation, typically social isolation. If there is more than one dog in a household, they may stimulate one another to bark.

Some dogs, especially those where there is some sort of fearfulness in their nature, may be more than usually noisy. Over-excitement, stress or conflict-related aspects of the home environment can be involved, and then there are causes due to owner behaviour and inadequate leadership, lack of obedience training, and encouraging barking where a dog has guard duties. Any of the above causes, if identifiable, should be tackled appropriately.

Treatment

Obedience training, plenty of exercise and socialization, increasing your dominance in the dog's eyes and delaying avoiding non-physical punishment are all of importance in every case of excessive and noisy vocalization. Physical punishment, as always, must never be used. Nor should you unintentionally reinforce the noise making by giving treats when it occurs. They will not act as a bribe but as reinforcers.

Punishment in the form of a scolding word or startling the dog with some other form of sound signal given at the time the barking occurs, can be combined with offering a reward for not doing it and, instead, responding immediately to your command to 'Sit!' or 'Stay!' At first give the command and then the reward as soon as the barking ceases on administering the scolding or sharp sound signal. Later you can proceed to give them at the moment the dog perceives the presence of some likely stimulus, and is about to bark but has not actually commenced.

I do not like the use of electric shock collars in dealing with undesirable behaviours, but a remote control collar, which delivers a sharp sound under your control, is perfectly acceptable in using the technique described above.

Surgery on the dog's vocal cords to stop persistent barking is practised in some countries, and some veterinarians are highly in favour of the practice. I regard it as a barbaric mutilation, which, thank goodness, is illegal in the United Kingdom. (I have been asked in the past to surgically de-bark sea lions to control their night-time honking and have always adamantly refused.)

SNIFFING, LICKING AND PESTERING PEOPLE

With their highly developed sense of smell, sniffing is a constant activity for dogs. Odours, for them, carry information pictures. They excel in detecting minute amounts of substances in the air or on surfaces to a degree far beyond human abilities. They can analyse the qualitative and quantitative nature of a large number of chemical compounds simultaneously, and remember them! They have been shown to be able to distinguish between individual human odours, between members of a single family and even between identical twins when both their odours were presented together.

The trouble is that some dogs take sniffing too far, ramming their noses into the groins of visitors or strangers in the street. What information they pick up down there I hesitate to imagine. Other wild carnivores are also enthusiastic sniffers and, kept in zoological collections, will continue to investigate human groins in the same way as dogs, if they get the opportunity. The most memorable example of this for me was a male Giant South American Otter, a magnificent specimen in the Zoo de la Casa de Campo, Madrid. Some years ago when making a routine visit, I was invited by Spanish television to say a few words to a camera crew filming a children's programme in the zoo, about these biggest and seldom exhibited of otters. I decided to do it by climbing down a ladder into the otter's 'riverbank' enclosure and then, standing a little distance from the animal, start spouting, with it in the background.

The otter, though unaccustomed to people descending into its domain, did not run off but, sniffing vigorously and simultaneously giving me a glimpse of its enormous fang teeth, at once made a steady beeline towards my groin. I began talking and the otter continued advancing, eyes fixed on my fly buttons and nostrils twitching violently. What possible scent messages could he possibly hope to glean from my trousers? Discretion being the better part of valour, I elected to flee when his fine head was six inches away. Wondering if I had been unnecessarily cowardly, I clambered back up the ladder while bidding a hurried 'adios' to the camera.

The following week, a painter working in the zoo did essentially what I had done, but without permission, during his lunch break. He slid his ladder down into the otter enclosure and descended to look at the animals. The male otter again sniffed his way earnestly towards this new visitor's groin, arrived there – and bit hard! The poor painter was rushed to hospital in possession of only one testicle.

Causes

Licking of other animals is a normal behaviour of the canid family. Mothers lick babies clean, pups, particularly of wild species, lick their mothers' mouths in the hope of stimulating the regurgitation of some food. Licking is also part of mutual grooming, and when it involves licking the genitals of another animal, as is commonly seen in wolf and African Hunting Dog packs, is a submissive act usually directed at a pack member higher in the hierarchy.

Again, the trouble arises when it occurs in domestic dogs in the family situation. Then, licking seems to be essentially a submissive act which, unintentionally, has been reinforced by the owner's behaviour, or, in other cases, it is an act of dominance designed to display the dog's superior niche, as he sees it, in the family pack hierarchy.

Pestering of visitors, usually non-aggressive and good-natured but persistent, and yet without any signs of submissiveness, is a nuisance, but not a serious one. It needs, nevertheless, to be corrected.

Treatment

These kinds of misbehaviour are usually easy to correct. Licking by a submissive pet will usually disappear if the owner always ignores it. Otherwise, and where the dog by its 'pushiness' seems to be asserting its dominance, control and leadership must be regained with other family members employing the same tactics. Obedience training is again the key. The dog must obey a few simple commands reliably. When he misbehaves after having been trained, interruption of the behaviour – by a sharp sound signal rather than a squirt from a water pistol, followed by a command and then a reward for obeying, is all that is necessary.

However, the timing of the three components – interruption/distraction, command and reward – is crucial. One must follow the other very closely, otherwise the reward may be taken as approval of the act of unwanted behaviour and thus a reinforcement of it. The final stage is to dispense with the distraction. A verbal command should be enough to deter your dog. Punishment is never appropriate in these cases.

ROLLING IN SMELLY MATERIAL

Many dogs delight in rolling in the smelliest things they come across – cow dung, a maggoty pigeon carcase, fox droppings (a favourite) and the like, never spring flowers or a bed of green herbs. They continue their walk and return home smelling appallingly. Why do they do it? Perhaps it recalls the ways of their ancestors who would mask their own scent in this manner when out hunting. Modern wolves and wild canid species are seen to roll in the dung of their prey. Smelling like a deer can make it easier to get close enough, undetected on the breeze, to catch a deer for supper.

Treatment

Preventing this unpleasant habit involves obedience training so that the dog can be called off when he is seen approaching a likely smelly object, together perhaps, with some form of distraction and, as usual, a reward for compliant good behaviour. Before going out on walks it can help to rub the dog down with a cloth carrying either his own or your body scent. This may work by giving him a sense of confidence in his own body odour. Some dogs, after being shampooed, will immediately go outside and roll in the grass or on soil and become a little grubby once more. The washing has removed their smell identity. Here again, rubbing them down with a cloth or piece of blanket carrying their scent will normally stop them doing this.

DRAGGING THE BOTTOM ALONG THE GROUND

Owners frequently complain of their dog 'wiping his bottom on the carpet', sometimes leaving a slight stain (known as scooting). Dogs of any age may suddenly do this, squatting down with their hind legs forward and under their bodies or splayed, and then dragging themselves along by means of their forefeet. This behaviour is not some bizarre psychological quirk but a simple physical one.

Causes and treatment

Some cases are due to the commonest canine tapeworm, *Dipylidium*, a parasite transmitted by fleas, in the dog's intestines. Segments of the tapeworm look very much like rice grains and they are capable of wriggling. If a worm is wriggling half in and half out of the dog's anus, the itch provoked may result in a 'scooting' display. The treatment is anti-tapeworm tablets from the vet or pet shop.

Other cases, however, are not due to parasites but involve irritation of one or both of the two anal glands (sometimes called anal sacs) that lie on either side of the anal opening. These glands produce the highly complex secretions which pass messages regarding hierarchical status, sexual matters, mental state, as well as much more that scientists have yet to fathom out, to other dogs. Sometimes the secretions clog up in the ducts of the glands or they become infected, again causing 'scooting' and repeated licking of the area. Blocked glands need to be emptied, although if they are swollen and painful it is best for a vet to see the animal in case there is an infection. Always have the glands emptied by a vet the first time this happens. If you'd like to do it yourself the next time it happens, ask the vet to show you how. Chronic or recurrent inflammation of the anal glands may require surgery to remove them once and for all.

MASTURBATION

We have all seen it, or something similar, happen. The vicar is sipping his tea with Grandma when up springs the old lady's dear little pooch, mounts the clergyman's outstretched pinstriped leg and begins to thrust away lustfully. 'He's an oversexed little bugger', 'He needs a mate', 'Too much red meat, I'd say' – I've heard the perplexed, often embarrassed, owners mutter such things so often over the years. Both male and female dogs may do it and the object of the mock-mating demonstration may be either a person or some inanimate item like a cushion or pillow, usually found to be one carrying the owner's scent.

Over-fussing of the dog is often a feature, the dog venting its frustration in this way when the owner is absent. Done while the owner is present, it again can be caused by giving the animal too much fondling attention or, conversely, little or no petting at all. Behaviourists claim that masturbation will never become an issue in later life if good obedience training is begun before puberty (around three to four months of age). As for the 'too much red meat' theory – a load of rubbish.

Treatment

Except in a very few cases of proven hormonal hypersexuality, castration or spaying is not the answer, nor is sending the animal off to indulge in mating. To correct this, all fondling must cease and you should concentrate on simple obedience training with reliable response to voice commands. When the dog begins to masturbate in front of you, he should be distracted from it – by throwing a ball or toy towards him – and then rewarded by lots of praise when he desists.

In households with young children, masturbation targeted at them can be a serious matter and one that is often highly disturbing for the child. If training does not quickly correct the behaviour it may be best to have the pet rehomed.

The dogs eat of the crumbs which
fall from their master's table.

GOSPEL OF ST. MATTHEW, XV, 27

FEEDING
PROBLEMS

12

One of the things that has changed most noticeably, particularly in recent years, as the dog has become domesticated, is its diet. Its wild cousins are still uncompromising carnivores, hunting, killing and consuming raw meat. In Africa, the hunting dog's principal prey are Thomson's gazelles and impala; North American wolves subsist almost entirely on caribou, elk, moose and deer; and the South American bush dog delights in feasting upon the semi-aquatic pacas, pursuing them into the water when they try to escape by swimming. Only the jackal is known to sometimes raid cultivated fruit crops and vegetable garbage as well as eating mushrooms and fallen fruit at certain seasons.

Our domestic dogs, via their owners, may be faced by a bewildering variety of processed foods containing meats of all kinds, vegetables, cereals and innumerable chemicals, and those that are fed on table scraps depend on their masters' gastronomic predilections. The specialist 'dog meat shops' that I remember as a boy in Lancashire are long gone. What a dog eats now is often what the TV advertisement raves about. Growing numbers of veterinary experts are now strongly advising owners to return to using a dog's 'evolutionary' diet, one that is based principally on raw, meaty bones. They insist that modern processed dog foods are a major cause of reproductive, dental and degenerative diseases in pets, including cancer, diabetes, arthritis and kidney failure.

In such circumstances, it is little wonder that some dogs develop food fads, fancies and, more importantly, nutritional problems that affect their health. They can become hooked, like their owners, on junk food and, if you take on such a pet, firmly set in its dietary preferences, it may take some time and much patience to correct matters.

DIET-RELATED BEHAVIOUR

Nowadays much attention is paid to the possibly undesirable effects of food additives on the behaviour of children. Many foodstuffs, not only 'junk food', contain E-number chemicals in the form of colourings, preservatives, sugars and the like. The same applies to pet food. I have a can of dog food in front of me bearing the words on the contents label 'EEC permitted colorants and additives'. I wonder who gives these 'permits' and how much they really know about the workings of the canine (and, for that matter, human) body. Some behaviour disorders in children have been attributed to food additives, and the same is true of dogs, with certain breeds appearing to be genetically more sensitive to particular additives. Preservatives may upset, for example, Cavalier King Charles Spaniels.

Cutting out additives

The protein, carbohydrate and vitamin content of diets can also affect dog behaviour. There is good evidence to show that reducing protein and increasing carbohydrates and vitamin B6 in an animal's diet will reduce certain types of aggressive behaviour although an increase in protein levels sometimes helps to quieten hyper-excitable pets. Vitamin E can help fend off the effects of senility on the brain. Hyperactive dogs, like hyperactive children, will often calm down if given

HOME COOKED DOG FOOD

NOTE: All quantities are per 10 kg dog weight.

$^2/_3$ cup rice

$^1/_3$ cup medium-fat meat

6 teaspoons raw liver

1 teaspoon steamed bone meal

1 teaspoon corn oil

$^1/_2$ teaspoon iodized salt

Boil the rice until tender and drain. Mince the meat and cook in a little water. Mix the two together, and then stir in the remaining ingredients. Feed either warm or cold.

food which is free of artificial colourings, flavourings, preservatives and sugars. How to test this? Do an experiment. Cut out canned food, which is usually high in protein, and dry food, which often contains lots of preservatives, and cook for your pet. Give him dishes such as boiled chicken, rabbit, lamb or fish mixed with boiled rice or mashed, unpeeled, boiled potatoes in the proportions of one part meat or fish to four parts rice or mash. If, within a week or two this diet does effect a change for the better in your dog's behaviour, go onto some form of low- but high-quality protein proprietary canned food that is claimed to be free of additives such as the ones recommended for animals with chronic kidney disease or low-protein organic ones. Alternatively, if you are prepared to continue with the home cooking, use the recipe above.

Vegetarian dogs

Vegetarian and even vegan proprietary foods for dogs are now available. Although in theory, at least, carnivores should take some meat in their diet, dogs on these meat-free menus do appear to thrive perfectly well. Nevertheless, it will be some years yet before we can be absolutely sure that there are no detrimental effects which might appear much later in a dog's life.

Elderly dogs

Earlier we discussed cognitive dysfunctional changes in the geriatric dog and the way in which certain additions, such as antioxidants, to the diet can produce improvements in behaviour. Some old dogs that 'forget' their house training will also benefit from having increased dietary choline, a nutrient found in many foods, which is available in tablet form from health food shops, and is used to reverse memory loss in human patients, as a daily supplement. Adding the amino-acid tryptophan to the diet can reduce the tendency to irascible behaviour in old dogs.

FINICKY EATERS

If the dog you have acquired is a fussy eater and you know little or nothing about the feeding regime at his previous home, don't worry too much so long as he is of normal weight and is not losing it gradually. If you have any doubts as to whether a poor appetite may be caused by some underlying medical condition, consult your vet without delay and also discuss suitable types and quantities of food.

Boosting your dog's appetite

There are several things you can do to try to increase a dog's appetite, and these are as follows:

- Cut down on titbit treats.
- Warm the food.
- If the proprietary food contains high levels of vegetable ingredients, switch to one with more meat of some sort.
- If using dry food, moisten it with warm water.
- Enhance the flavour of the food by adding some meat gravy, chicken stock, cooked grated garlic, roast pork crackling, half a teaspoonful of dried yeast powder or a little tinned cat food (some dogs find it more tasty than the canine equivalents).
- Add a small amount of freshly cooked meat, such as liver, kidney, sausage or roast chicken skin, to the food. If it works, gradually reduce the quantity.
- Feed little and often.

OBSESSIVE DRINKING OF WATER

Dogs that seem to be continually drinking (and consequently having to urinate frequently) are usually suffering from one of almost two dozen possible physical ailments, such as sugar diabetes, water diabetes, kidney disease, adrenal gland malfunction or, in females, pyometra (a serious condition of the uterus). Some such dogs, however, are not physically ill. Their exaggerated desire for water is psychological: so-called psychogenic polydipsia. For the owner, it is the increased need to urinate rather than the drinking that creates a nuisance. It is essential for all abnormally thirsty dogs to be examined by a vet. Blood and urine tests and possibly other diagnostic techniques will be required. Only if all the pathological causes of such behaviour can be ruled out, will the case be considered behavioural.

WATER TIP

Some experts believe that it is best not to give chlorinated or fluorine treated water to hyperactive dogs, but to provide bottled still mineral water instead.

Treatment

Handling such dogs entails instilling basic obedience to voice commands through simple training, distracting them in some manner when they start imbibing, as described for other unwanted behaviours, followed by a command to do something else, and a reward promptly given upon compliance.

For some dogs an excellent distraction is putting them in kennels for a few days, provided your vet is satisfied that there is no disease underlying the behaviour. Denying the animal access to water is cruel whatever the nature of the case, and dangerous, possibly fatal, if some physical cause is involved.

OBESITY

It is said that there is nowadays an epidemic of obesity among the human population in the United States, Great Britain and some other Western countries, and it would seem that carrying far too much fat is now literally 'going to the dogs' as well. Over one-quarter of all the pet dogs in the USA are overweight, and you will not be surprised to learn that obese owners are far more likely to have obese dogs than those of lighter build. Clearly, if you prefer to sit and watch TV munching burgers and doughnuts and drinking sweet colas or beer for hours on end, the dog at your feet, who you love to bits and take care to ensure has a brimming food bowl nearby at all times, will, more than likely, come to look like you. Obesity is never seen in the dog's wild relatives; indeed wolves always seem to me to be the epitome of the 'lean and hungry look'.

But what is the definition of an obese dog? The best definition, I think, is one where the animal is at least 20 per cent heavier than its ideal weight. Keeping a dog at its ideal weight is considered to extend its life expectancy by as much as 15 per cent so taking control of his weight is essential.

WHICH BREEDS TEND TO BE OVERWEIGHT?

Some breeds seem to become over-plump more readily than others. They include the Shetland Sheepdog, Dachshund, Labrador, Basset Hound, Beagle and Cocker Spaniel. Breeds that are less likely to put on unwanted pounds are the Greyhound, Whippet, Boxer and German Shepherd. Not surprisingly, working dogs like Border Collies and hunting terriers generally retain good figures throughout their lives.

Effects on health

For both man and dogs, obesity is dangerous and capable of causing a wide range of health problems. In dogs the effects of any arthritis in old age are much worsened and there is an increased incidence of heart disease, diabetes and breathing difficulties. Some medical conditions, such as thyroid and adrenal gland malfunction and diabetes can not only result from, but also actually cause obesity. Reducing the weight of an obese dog, or human, with joint afflictions such as osteo-arthritis, is one of the most effective aids in treatment.

The older your dog, the more chance of him tending to put on excessive weight. Obesity is commoner in bitches and neutered animals of both sexes than in entire males and bitches. Bitches given long-term contraceptive treatment with drugs such as megestrol often have increased appetites and become too heavy.

Treatment

Your newly inherited pet may arrive already too fat. It is your responsibility to trim him down or, if he is not yet obese, prevent him ever becoming so. Fighting canine obesity is out of the hands (paws) of the animal itself. It is you, the owner, who chooses the quantity and quality of your dog's food and who provides, or does not provide, adequate opportunities for calorie-burning exercise. Exercising a dog is a superb slimming aid for both you and your pet. So, here we have a situation where it is not the dog that needs re-training but the owner. How to go about it?

As well as regular daily exercise of some sort, which should be increased gradually and steadily as the dog becomes fitter and leaner, correct diet is essential. It is important to keep the dog's calorie intake under control. If a young dog's daily rations contain merely one per cent more calories than are needed for bodily maintenance, he will be 25 per cent overweight by the time he reaches middle age. Below are some useful guidelines for tackling obesity in your dog.

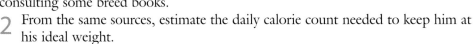

Play is a valuable form of exercise and can be used to control weight and improve health and vitality.

1. Find out your dog's ideal weight by asking your vet or breeder or consulting some breed books.

2. From the same sources, estimate the daily calorie count needed to keep him at his ideal weight.

3. Estimate the calorie content (there are plenty of calorie tables available for human use) of all the foodstuffs you propose to give him.

4. Now work out a daily diet containing only 60 per cent of the number of calories you calculated as being right to maintain his ideal weight.

5. Split the daily amount into two feeds. By this means most obese dogs will safely lose about 250 g (8 oz) per week, reaching their target weight in about three months. If you find any of this confusing, the veterinary nurses in your local practice will be only too willing to assist.

6. If possible, stop all food treats or change them to pieces of cooked vegetable or meat gravy ice cubes.

7. Consider a diet of proprietary canned or dry slimming foods.

8 If giving dry food, ensure that, for a reasonably active dog, it contains no more than 16 per cent fat; for a more sedentary type, no more than 12 per cent.

9 Cut back on meal and biscuits. Instead, give green beans, carrots and other root vegetables. Keep the protein content to between 20 and 40 per cent.

10 When doing your initial calorie calculations, don't forget to include estimates for any table scraps and treats you may feed.

NOTE: For the old dog, turn to page 81 for advice on their particular dietary requirements.

Slimming classes

Many veterinary clinics run excellent programmes for weight reduction in pets, a sort of Dog's Weight Watchers. An initial visit will include a full health check up, weighing, usually by a veterinary nurse, and planning an appropriate diet and exercise regime for the particular dog, and one that fits in with the owner's capabilities. Regular repeat visits must be made to monitor progress in weight loss, adjust the regime if necessary and sort out any problems that might have arisen. Progress, confirmed by the veterinary clinic, acts as an enormous encouragement to the owner who sees steady change in the appearance and vitality of the dog.

A recent innovation is the 'dog gym' where pets, and at the same time in many cases, their owners, can get fit and lose unwanted pounds through supervised courses of exercise. If it is true that owners take after their pets, it is certainly worth pursuing whatever course is the most successful to get yourself and your dog into shape, and the motivation to keep fit is all the more potent, when the real health benefits such as added energy and improved well-being, start to show.

CASE HISTORY OBESE DOGS

Barney was a six-year-old Alaskan Malamute tipping the scales at 80 kg (175 lb), twice his ideal weight of around 40 kg (88 lb). The extra load his body carried around had damaged his joints and he could only manage to walk a few paces before collapsing, breathless. Even then, lying down created its problems. The under-surfaces of his chest and legs were covered with 'bed sore' type ulcers.

By good fortune, rescued by a concerned dog lover, Barney was enrolled in the slimming programme run by the local village veterinary clinic, and every two weeks he was carefully monitored. One year later the Malamute was a totally different creature. Weighing 38 kg, running more than walking, and rather pushy in insisting his wise new owner bring the lead without delay, so that they could set out on their daily constitutional over the moorland, he looked superb.

EATING DROPPINGS

The oft-reported canine taste for eating faeces (coprophagia) is regarded by dog owners as the most bizarre and unpleasant of problem behaviours. Before we scoff too much, however, it is worth recalling that the rarest and most expensive coffee in the world, Kopi Luwak, an Indonesian brand that, when available, costs a small fortune and is avidly consumed by humans, particularly in Japan, is made from beans that have been eaten and then defecated not, as is often claimed, by monkeys but by the small carnivore called the palm civet.

Causes

The habit seems to be commoner in bitches than in dogs and can involve eating the animal's own faeces or those of another dog or another species. Puppies' stools are normally eaten by their mother as a hygienic measure, but the reasons for coprophagia in other adult dogs are not understood. In some cases it may be related to underlying intestinal parasitism or pancreatic disease interfering with digestion. Other theories mooted by behaviourists have included attention getting, a canine preference for decaying food (not one I'm familiar with) and, with particular regard to the eating of horse dung, as a food source when more normal victuals are in scarce supply. I am not enamoured of any of these propositions, and have long preferred the possibility that it is caused by a deficiency of some necessary element in the affected dog's diet.

Treatment

To correct the behaviour, try changing the dog's diet to one that is high in fibre and protein but low in carbohydrates. A daily dose of a proprietary multi-vitamin/iron/trace element preparation obtainable from your vet, pharmacist or pet shop, should also be given.

Most dogs defecate immediately after eating so you should supervise this and give a sharp sound signal as soon as your dog has produced the stools and distract him immediately into some pleasurable activity. Praise him lavishly while, at the same time, drawing him away from the faeces. Take him indoors and then return to dispose of the stools. Note also that applying some hot pepper sauce to stools can be effective when a dog eats them during long periods of confinement.

If your dog attempts to consume faeces when out for a walk, either studiously ignore the behaviour (effective if in some way you have

Once the dog has defecated, distract him and gently lead him away from the faeces to prevent any being eaten.

unintentionally reinforced the behaviour in the past) or, if that fails, scold him, ideally while pulling him away by means of a halter and lead.

SWALLOWING OTHER NON-FOOD ITEMS

One common surgical procedure performed on dogs by veterinarians is gastrotomy: opening up the stomach to extract a foreign body that may already be causing signs of obstruction. All sorts of objects from stones to jewellery to ladies' underwear have been removed in this way. My strangest haul from a dog, a German Shepherd, was a mouth organ, though for sheer quantity of foreign material nothing beats the one-and-a-half bucketsful of assorted stones that I took from the stomach of a Californian sea lion living in a Yorkshire zoo. Before the operation one could hear a crunching sound like someone walking across shingle when it moved about on land. Sea lions and dolphins, like domestic dogs, not uncommonly develop the habit of swallowing foreign bodies (known as pica). Whereas the former tend to specialize in stones, the latter can get into trouble through filling up their first stomachs with tightly-pressed balls of leaves, particularly in the autumn.

Causes

It is difficult to explain what dogs get out of swallowing seemingly untasty items, such as socks or wristwatches. On the first occasion it could be accidental, but why keep on doing it? Maybe the act of just gobbling down relieves stress in some way. Dogs that eat stones and the like may begin by simply investigating the item by mouthing it. This leads on to swallowing, either as attention seeking or where the owner reinforces the act by behaving in a concerned manner, perhaps running after the animal to try to retrieve the object.

Treatment

Some dogs will quickly gobble down the object as their owner approaches. In that case, don't do it. Ignore the dog. That may suffice, but where the dog swallows the object even though being ignored, he should be trained to pick up and/or hold things and then drop them on command with suitable immediate reward. Also effective is interrupting the dog at the moment he approaches the object by means of a hand clap or other sound signal, followed by a distraction of some sort and a reward for immediate compliance (see page 108).

You should also check out your dog's feeding regime. Is he receiving enough food at regular meal times? Dogs, particularly elderly ones, need to be fed twice a day. Finally, the dog's favourite swallowing objects can be sprinkled with chilli pepper powder as a simple aversion therapy.

To be, contents his natural desire,
He asks no angel's wing, no seraph's fire;
But thinks, admitted to that equal sky,
His faithful dog shall bear him company.

POPE, LETTERS TO H.CROMWELL 1709

POSTCRIPT

To summarize what we have discussed in this book, the main points to remember when acquiring a new dog from whatever source, in order to establish a happy relationship and a peaceful life together for both you and your dog are as follows:

◆ Obedience training is of primary importance.

◆ You must have a positive, leading approach to your dog, not a negative, punitive one.

◆ All members of your family must behave consistently and in the same manner as one another towards the dog.

◆ A pleasant, stress-free environment for the dog is essential.

◆ The dog must be given adequate regular exercise and play time.

◆ A good, balanced diet with supplementation at certain times of life must be provided.

◆ Take your dog for a regular veterinary health check: yearly for young dogs, six monthly for old timers, or as advised by the vet.

INDEX

CREDITS

SPECIAL PHOTOGRAPHY: © Octopus Publishing Group/Geoff Langan.

ALL OTHER PHOTOGRAPHY: Alamy/Jack Cox/Travel Pics Pro 27; /Guy Edwardes Photography 13; /Francisco Martinez 15. Bourne Publishing Group/Your Dog Magazine 52. Getty Images/Kim Wolhuter 35. Octopus Publishing Group Limited/Steve Gorton 8, 14 centre right, 45 top, 45 bottom, 46 top right, 47, 90, 93, 120; /Rosie Hyde 18, 76; /Peter Loughran 16 top; /Ray Moller 12, 14 top left, 16 bottom; /Angus Murray 40, 85, 107, 128, 132; /Tim Ridley 99, 112, 153, 155. Photodisc 11. Warren Photographic/Jane Burton 32-33, 44.

ACKNOWLEDGEMENTS

MANY THANKS TO THE TEAM at Cassell Illustrated, in particular my superb editor, Joanne Wilson, and to Anna Cheifetz, Publishing Manager, Auberon Hedgecoe, Art Director, and to our designer Austin Taylor, as well as my good friend and pug fancier, Project Editor, Heather Thomas. Their hard work and expertise has made this book what it is.

THANKS ALSO TO PHOTOGRAPHER, Geoff Langan, dog handler and advisor, Sandra Strong, and Liz Fowler, Jennifer Veall, Sophie Delpech, and Sue Bosanko.

THANKS TO HYDROVET for the life-jackets. 664a Wandsworth Road, London.

THANK YOU TO COMPANY OF ANIMALS for supplying many of the toys and training equipment. Website is at <www.companyofanimals.co.uk>.

HUMAN MODELS APPEARING INCLUDE: father and daughter, Jake and Eill, the Bradley family, Danielle DiMichiel, Heather Thomas and Daisy Hutchison.

DOGS (IN ORDER OF APPEARANCE) INCLUDE: Charlie (*cover model*), 13, a Bassett Hound, is a star of magazines, advertising and training videos. She is a real-life rescue dog, badly abused in her past but now safe, despite still having a pin in her leg; Florence (*page 1*), 7-year-old Jack Russell terrier, is famous for many television appearances, magazines and even the catwalk, and has appeared with Rolf Harris; Beetle (*page 2*) is a 12½-year-old Black Labrador – fashion model and television star; Jasper (*page 4*), 4-year-old Wire hair miniature dachshund, loves children and other puppies star of fashion shoots. He plays with Saffy a baby Pug – this is her first appearance in print. Leo (*page 7*), 4, is a Golden-Retriever star of countless magazine shoots, TV, and training videos; Goldie (page 53), 10, a Golden Retriever, has appeared on many TV and training videos; Hank (*page 59*), 9, is a White German Shepherd and star of fashion shoots; Peig, (*page 59*) 13, a cross-breed, based in Somerset; Bull, (*page 64*), a 10-year-old Pakistani Street Dog; Dolly, (*page 79*), 3, Norfolk Terrier and star of advertising; Spence, 3, is a wire-hair dachshund (*page 123*). For more information on these and other models visit <www.dogs-on-camera.com>.

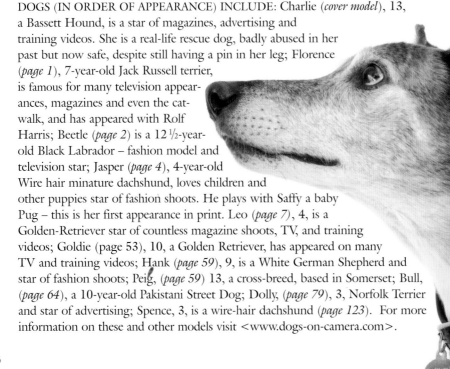